The Doctrine and Administration of the Church

The Doctrine and Administration of the Church

Paul R. Jackson

REGULAR BAPTIST PRESS
1300 North Meacham Road
Post Office Box 95500
Schaumburg, Illinois 60195

Library of Congress Cataloging in Publication Data

Jackson, Paul Rainey, 1903-1969
    The doctrine and administration of the church.

    Bibliography: p. 191
    1.   Regular Baptists—Doctrinal and controversial
works.   I.   Title.
BX6389.7.J3 1979   230'.8'61   79-25015
ISBN 0-87227-072-6

THE DOCTRINE AND ADMINISTRATION OF THE CHURCH

To my wife
who, throughout my ministry,
has been an inspiration
and a faithful and capable partner
in the Lord's work

Contents

Contents

Foreword

"HE . . . YET SPEAKETH."

How well I remember reading page after page of the handwritten copy of this book as it came from Dad's pen a number of years ago. He always loved the church, and his churches loved him. Later, as President of Baptist Bible Seminary and National Representative of the General Association of Regular Baptist Churches, he was one of the most respected and loved men in the ranks of fundamentalism. I was proud of him.

He often said that a local church was the hardest thing in the world to kill. You can maim it, wound it, bleed it and do it injustice—but it's hard to kill it because it is a divine institution and Christ is its Head!

Dad's clear thinking about spiritual things, about the operation of the church, about the doctrine of the church, brought this book into being. Now it is accepted in many places as a standard work on local church administration.

The Laodicean lukewarmness predicted to come on the church has fallen upon us. In areas of both polity and doctrine, the terrible declension has come. Churches have no deep-seated convictions about the Word of God; pastors are compromisers and opportunists; laymen in the pew have been deeply infected by worldliness.

Against this bleak but predicted condition is the bright promise that such lethargy marks the time of the Lord's return. In light of that, the true church of Jesus Christ, represented by faithful, Bible-believing Baptist churches, must determinedly submit to the lordship of Jesus Christ and honor Him with every fiber of their being. The content of this book, if studied and applied in the churches, will enhance faithfulness in our polity and clarity in our doctrine.

I sincerely trust that the perpetuation of my father's life, ministry and convictions through the means of the revision of this book will be a blessing to all who study it.

— *Mark Jackson*
President, Baptist Bible College
and School of Theology
Clarks Summit, Pennsylvania

1

The Church
Which Is His Body

GOD NEVER CHANGES (Mal. 3:6; James 1:17), although His dealings with men have changed during the ages. From Abraham to Christ, His relationship with men centered in the nation of Israel. Since Christ, His ministry has been through the Church. Israel, as a nation, has been set aside until the Church is raptured (Rom. 11:25). For fifteen hundred years before Christ, the law given through Moses was in force. Since Christ, the Scriptures declare that we are not under law but under grace (Rom. 6:14; see also John 1:17).

This does not mean there are two ways of salvation. God has never saved men by works in any age. Faith in Him has been the universal qualification. Shed blood has been the unvarying requirement. Before Christ, animal sacrifices were offered at the command of God. Sin was thereby acknowledged and covered (Lev. 17:11; Heb. 10:1-4). Then Christ came and died for our sins. He died for the sins that were past (Rom. 3:25) and redeemed those who were under the law (Gal. 4:4, 5).

So while God does not change and salvation has always been by faith in Him, God did an entirely new thing when He established the Church. The distinctions between law and grace, Israel and the Church, must be clearly discerned if the Word of God is to be understood.

The Scripture also distinguishes between the Church which is the Body of Christ (Eph. 1:22, 23) and local churches. The local church is the current practical manifestation of the Body of Christ. The local church is the major emphasis of the New Testament. The Greek word *ekklesia,* translated church, is applied to the local churches some ninety times, and to the Church which is His Body about twenty times.

Sometimes referred to as the universal or the invisible Church, the

Church which is His Body is a blessed fact, emphasizing the unity of God's people in this age. It includes all the redeemed, whether Jews or Gentiles, from Pentecost to the Rapture, whether in Heaven or on earth. It never meets during this age. It makes no decisions, exercises no discipline, administers no ordinances and preaches no gospel. It is awaiting completion when it will finally be gathered in Glory as "the general assembly and church of the firstborn . . ." (Heb. 12:23).

The local New Testament church is often dishonored by referring to the Church which is His Body as "the true church," thus inferring that a local church is not a true church. It is a true church if established according to the Word of God. The terminology which refers to the Body as an organism and the local church as an organization needs to be used carefully lest the false inference be given that the organization is man-made and unimportant.

If these distinctions are clearly seen so that the local church is not robbed of its significant position, the truth concerning the Church which is His Body encourages and comforts.

An undue emphasis has been placed in our present day on so-called "body truth." It has resulted in minimizing the local church upon which the Scriptures major.

Some people refuse to obey certain Scriptures that command the discipline of disobedient brethren. They magnify the truth of our relationship to each other in His Body out of proportion to the Biblical commands to maintain a pure local church (1 Cor. 5). This imbalance of truth has also caused a tragic disregard of New Testament churches so that many persons consider baptism and church membership as non-essentials. Some have virtually become church tramps, without any local responsibility in attendance, stewardship or discipline. This is a serious situation and should arouse us to our tasks in our own churches as we follow the Word of God.

The Lord help us to love all our brethren in Christ, wherever they are or whatever they are doing. We ought to seek their welfare, fellowship with them when it is possible and pray for them earnestly. This relationship, however, never justifies our participation with them in disobedience. Many Biblical commands like the following are amply clear: "Now we command you, brethren, in the name of our Lord Jesus Christ, that ye withdraw yourselves from every brother that walketh disorderly, and not after the tradition which he received of us" (2 Thess. 3:6). These "traditions" certainly seem to refer to all the oral and written apostolic ministry of that day. (See 2 Thessalonians 2:15.) It is not Biblical, therefore, as many argue, to have fellowship with all men simply because they are saved, or claim to be. Even though they are saved and we shall spend eternity with them in Glory, we are not authorized to spend the present with them in their disobedience. (See Matthew 18:15-17.) This is a truth which every born-again believer needs ever to bear in mind.

By refusing to fellowship with others within His Body, one of the divine objectives is that such ones should be delivered from disobedience and restored to fellowship. This is evident in the judgment imposed in 1 Corinthians 5:5 and the subsequent forgiveness in 2 Corinthians 2:6-11. It is our responsibility to seek such deliverance for a brother (Gal. 6:1), but we are never justified in fellowshipping with him in his sin. To do such a thing is definitely forbidden by God's Word and is thus to be shunned by every born-again believer.

The Church Purposed

The Church is repeatedly called the Body of Christ (Eph. 1:22, 23). We shall consider the significance of this terminology later. It is this Body, the Church, of which Paul writes in Ephesians 3. Read verses 1-12. Here the Church is called the "mystery of Christ," which in other ages was not made known, but is now revealed. The unique feature, entirely new in this age, is: "That the Gentiles should be fellowheirs [with the Jews], and of the same body, and partakers of his promise in Christ by the gospel" (v. 6).

This Church was born in the eternal purpose of God (v. 11), and this mystery was hid in God from the beginning of the world (v. 9). Jesus Christ began the unveiling of that purpose when He said, "I will build my church" (Matt. 16:18). The apostle Paul was chosen to be the primary channel of revelation of this mystery (Eph. 3:1-4), although he declares (v. 5) that "it is now revealed unto his holy apostles and prophets by the Spirit."

The claims made by some extreme dispensationalists are obviously false when they declare that Paul was the single source of revelation and that he knew nothing of this mystery until his Prison Epistles (Ephesians, Philippians, Colossians, 2 Timothy and Philemon). Not only did he say that the Spirit revealed this truth to holy apostles and prophets (plural), but he himself knew this truth early in his ministry. See 1 Corinthians 12:13: "For by one spirit are we all baptized into one body, whether we be Jews or Gentiles, whether we be bond or free; and have been all made to drink into one Spirit."

In Ephesians 3 it is evident that God planned and purposed the Church throughout eternity, but He did not reveal it until this age. It is perfectly natural that this should be true! God is a reasonable Being with all wisdom and power. We change our plans and make new ones because we do not know the future and have very limited understanding. But this is not true with God, Who has never been surprised or defeated. He "worketh all things after the counsel of his own will" (Eph. 1:11). The "blueprint" of the ages has always existed in His infinite, unchanging intelligence. How comforting this is to the believer as the ages unfold. Our Lord is "the Father of Eternity" (Isa. 9:6, ASV footnote).

God's eternal purpose to build the Church did not center merely in the salvation of souls, although that is a glorious aspect of this work. He purposed the Church from all eternity that in it might be seen the riches of His grace (Eph. 2:7) and the greatness of His wisdom (Eph. 3:10), and that Christ thereby might have the preeminence so rightfully His (Col. 1:18).

That He should choose us to fulfill such lofty counsels should humble our hearts and lead us to adore and worship at His feet.

The Church Pictured

No revelation of the Church is given in the Old Testament. However, now that it has been revealed in the New Testament, it becomes evident by the word pictures of the Old Testament that this new creation was in the mind of God, Who is the Author of the whole Bible. The things that happened to Israel were designed of God to provide examples for us (1 Cor. 10:11). The Tabernacle, the offerings and the priesthood are rich with "life-size object lessons" of Biblical truths. Christ and His work are pictured in types and shadows of the Old Testament (Col. 2:16, 17).

No Christian can afford to neglect the study of the Old Testament along with the New. God is the Author of both portions. As someone said long ago: "The New is in the Old contained; the Old is in the New explained."

We suggest three well-known examples which picture the Bride, another figure used to describe the Church in our relationship to Christ.

1. With the New Testament revelation in Ephesians 5:29-32 before us, it is clear that in Genesis 2:21-24 we have an Old Testament picture of the Church, the Bride of Christ.

As God caused a deep sleep to come upon Adam, and then from his opened side took the material from which his bride was made; so God caused the deep sleep of death to fall upon the "last Adam" (1 Cor. 15:45), and from His pierced side came forth the blood for the redemption of His Bride.

The parallel continues as Adam says of Eve: "This is now bone of my bones, and flesh of my flesh . . . ," and of Christ and the Church we read: "For we are members of his body, of his flesh, and of his bones" (Eph. 5:30). Thus is the parallel drawn in Scripture.

2. In Genesis 24 Abraham sent his servant into a far country to secure a bride for his only son, Isaac (Gen. 22:12). Many interesting details of this delightful narrative suggest the blessed ministry of the Spirit, Who has come into the world to secure the Bride for Christ.

The picture does not present the thought of our redemption. It does suggest, however, that the Bride must be born of the proper family! The servant was obligated to take a bride from Abraham's kindred, not from the Canaanites. He therefore did not determine that Rebekah was the bride for Isaac until he knew her family origin (Gen. 24:24, 26, 47, 48). So must we be of God's family to be the Bride of Christ. Unless by the new birth we are partakers of the divine nature, we shall never share the glories of the Heavenly Bridegroom.

Another significant aspect of this picture is the way in which this unnamed servant skillfully directed Rebekah's affection to Isaac. He told her of Isaac (Gen. 24:33-45) and how he inherited the greatness and riches of his father, Abraham. He began from the first to shower upon her some of the riches of his master that he had brought with him to this far country. Though she had never seen Isaac, he was so presented to her that her heart went out to him; and when asked for a decision, she promptly replied, "I will go." So does the Spirit of God woo for Christ those whom God has chosen for Him. We learn of His greatness, we receive of His bounties, until, without compulsion but with wills transformed, we gladly say, "I will go!"

We point out only one other similarity. As Isaac came out of the house into the field at the end of the day, the servant had completed his mission and was bringing Rebekah to him from her old home. As they met, he took her back to his father's home as his wife. The blessed hope of the Church lies at the evening of this day of grace when the Lord Jesus will leave the place God is now preparing in the Father's house (John 14:1-3; 1 Thess. 4:16, 17). He will descend into the air to meet His Bride that the Spirit of God will then have completed and prepared to meet Him. Together they shall return to the Father's house and to the marriage of the Lamb!

3. Many truths are revealed in the Book of Ruth, and among them is the story of the kinsman-redeemer who redeemed for himself a bride from among the Moabites. No Spirit-taught heart can miss here the picture of the One Who was made flesh so He could redeem us and make us His Bride.

According to the law of the kinsman-redeemer as stated in Leviticus 25:25-55 and Deuteronomy 25:5-10, it was the God-given duty of the one "nearest of kin" to redeem the land or the person of a relative who, because of poverty or other reason, had been seized by another party. In addition, if a husband died without an heir, it was the duty of the brother, or next nearest relative, to marry the widow and raise up a child to perpetuate the name of the dead husband.

In order to become our Kinsman-Redeemer, the Lord Jesus was made flesh. (See Hebrews 2:14-18; Galatians 4:4, 5; Ephesians 5:23-27.) The law, which was weak through the flesh (Rom. 8:3), was unable to produce life; and now we are dead to that law in order that we might be married to another, "even to him who is raised from the dead, that we should bring forth fruit unto God" (Rom. 7:4).

All this is pictured in the lovely story of Ruth and her kinsman-redeemer, Boaz. Read the entire book, especially the fourth chapter.

Obviously there is not enough detail in these narratives to have prematurely revealed God's purpose. But there is sufficient to indicate the delighted anticipation of God as He contemplated that purpose and waited until the appointed time.

The Church Promised

Jesus Christ, the Creator and Sustainer of all things, came into the world to undertake the work of a new creation. As He stood on the threshold of the accomplishment of that eternal purpose, He declared, "I will build my church . . ." (Matt. 16:18).

The events that followed seemed to threaten the fulfillment of this promise. Men forsook Him. Peter denied Him. The enemies captured Him. Fetters, trials, a cross, a tomb—these appeared to contradict His promise. But His words were pure words. He could not deny Himself. Wicked men who crucified Him did not know; but God knew that "except a corn of wheat fall into the ground and die, it abideth alone: but if it die, it bringeth forth much fruit" (John 12:24).

He arose from death triumphant, as the Head of the new creation. Redeemed with His blood and undergirded by His resurrection power, the Church was now to appear. His promise would be fulfilled.

The promise of the Church relates not only to its origin, but to its preservation. Christ said, "I will build my church; and the gates of hell shall not prevail against it" (Matt. 16:18). He has promised that satanic opposition will not overthrow His people individually, or His Church corporately, in this age (1 Pet. 1:3-7). However, this statement in Matthew seems to go beyond that, promising that even death itself will not triumph over the Church. The gates of a city do not invade or conquer an enemy. Hell here is "hades," the place of the departed dead. Literally, therefore, the promise is that death itself will not prevail against the Church. As members of the church at Thessalonica died, the Thessalonians seemed disturbed over this very problem. They were comforted and instructed thus: "But I would not have you to be ignorant, brethren, concerning them which are asleep, that ye sorrow not, even as others which have no hope. For if we believe that Jesus died and rose again, even so them also which sleep in Jesus will God bring with him" (1 Thess. 4:13, 14).

He has promised not only to build but also to preserve the Church for all eternity.

The Church Purchased

Self-righteous men are consistently seeking to secure God's favor and a place in Heaven through things they give or things they do. Nothing could be more futile, as is evident from Titus 3:5; Ephesians 2:8 and 9; Romans 4:4 and 5; and similar portions.

God condemns with awful finality any other way of salvation because Christ provided the one perfect way. Any other way is an insult to our Lord Jesus Who is the Way; and God will not tolerate any other (Gal. 1:8, 9; Prov. 14:12; John 3:36). An infinite price has already been paid for our redemption with the precious blood of Christ, and it is blasphemy to seek to substitute another "price," or to supplement that price with our own contribution as though His blood was insufficient. To us who are saved, Peter writes: "Ye know that ye were not redeemed with corruptible things, as silver and gold . . . But with the precious blood of Christ . . ." (1 Pet. 1:18, 19).

Why must it be the blood of Christ to accomplish our redemption? Many are not clear in their conception of this matter. *It must be blood* because the life is in the blood (Lev. 17:11), and the righteousness and justice of God require a life for a life if we are to be redeemed. He took my place and became my Substitute: ". . . Christ died for the ungodly" (Rom. 5:6). When His blood was shed, He gave His life in place of mine under God's judgment for sin. *It must be Christ's blood,* for all others have sinned and would die for their own sin. Furthermore, because He is God, His blood is of infinite value (it is precious blood!), and He is the propitiation not for our sins only, but also for the sins of the whole world (1 John 2:2). No wonder we delight to sing:

Redeemed—how I love to proclaim it!
Redeemed by the blood of the Lamb;

Redeemed through His infinite mercy—
His child, and forever, I am.

This redemptive act of God was necessary if He was to save men, for we had sinned and were sold under sin. When He gave Himself for us, it was so He could redeem us from all iniquity (Titus 2:14). Redemption through His blood brought about our deliverance from "the power of darkness" and our translation into the kingdom of His dear Son (Col. 1:13, 14). The death of Christ is also the instrument for the destruction of the Devil and the deliverance of "them who through fear of death were all their lifetime subject to bondage" (Heb. 2:14, 15). Therefore, the precious blood of Christ is the only price of redemption which God will recognize. It fully and finally delivers every believer from the judgment of God which should rightfully have fallen upon us who were sold under sin, characterized by iniquity and subject to the bondage of Satan and the power of darkness.

In paying this redemption as He died upon the cross, the Savior satisfied the righteous claims of a holy God. Justice was meted out to a willing Substitute; sin was thereby brought into judgment; and God was just in His justification of the ungodly (Rom. 3:23-26). The redemption is not paid to Satan to release us, as some have erroneously taught, but is necessary to the satisfying of divine justice. God has willed to bring every sin into judgment. This He must do for He is holy. It will necessitate that every man who neglects or rejects the redemption provided in the precious blood of Christ will fall under His eternal condemnation.

In His death the Lord Jesus loved us and gave Himself for us as individuals. But He also had in mind the purpose of the Church, as declared in Ephesians 5:25: ". . . Christ also loved the church, and gave himself for it." Acts 20:28 speaks of "the church of God, which he hath purchased with his own blood." We, therefore, belong to Him and, as Paul says, are espoused or betrothed to one husband—that is, to Christ (2 Cor. 11:1-3). Certainly we ought to be faithful to our Lord and love Him in word and in truth. We are to love Him with a pure and undiluted love. We are not to love the world or the things that are in the world. The wife who forsakes the love of her husband and gives her affections to another is contemptible before God and man. So also is the Church when she forsakes the love of Christ. The Word speaks with terrible bluntness upon this subject: "Ye adulterers and adulteresses, know ye not that the friendship of the world is enmity with God? whosoever therefore will be a friend of the world is the enemy of God" (James 4:4).

The world crucified our Savior and still tramples under its feet the precious blood of Christ. This fact fully justifies the awful denunciation of those who profess to love Christ, but who are the friends of the world. The Lord help us never to fall into such base ingratitude!

The Church Produced

The Church was purposed in the mind of God throughout the eternal ages; it was pictured in the Old Testament; it was promised by Jesus Christ during His earthly ministry; and it was purchased on the cross of Calvary. It was not produced, however, as a living reality until the Day of Pentecost, fifty days after the resurrection of Christ.

The time of the creation of the Church is indicated in the following Scripture: (1) the Church is the Body of Christ (Eph. 1:22, 23); (2) the Body is formed by the baptism of the Holy Spirit (1 Cor. 12:13); (3) the disciples had not been baptized with the Holy Spirit at the time of Christ's ascension into Heaven, but were then promised, ". . . Ye shall be baptized with the Holy Ghost not many days hence" (Acts 1:5). Ten days later, this took place; the Church which is His Body came into being.

The words in John 7:38 and 39 are significant in this connection: ". . . The Holy Ghost was not yet given; because that Jesus was not yet glorified." While the Spirit was always here in the sense of His omnipresence, He was promised in a new and different sense when the Lord Jesus said, "And I will pray the Father, and he shall give you another Comforter, that he may abide with you for ever; Even the Spirit of truth . . ." (John 14:16, 17).

This age of the Church is often called the age of the Holy Spirit because of the distinctive relationship which He bears to the redeemed in this age. He now abides with us; and "if any man have not the Spirit of Christ, he is none of his" (Rom. 8:9). Our bodies are the temples of the Holy Spirit which we have of God, as Paul writes in 1 Corinthians 6:19.

The baptism of the Holy Spirit is not to be confused with the indwelling of the Spirit, and yet the two cannot be separated. When He indwelt the believers on the Day of Pentecost, He also united them into an organic unit called the Body of Christ. The Body has many members but is one Body (1 Cor. 12:12), and Christ is the Head (Eph. 4:15, 16).

Men who believed were saved during the Old Testament ages and also during the earthly ministry of Christ. Apart from the national unity of Israel and her covenant relationship to God, men did not then enjoy any such unity with each other and the Lord as has come to pass with the creation of the Church. This blessed experience is ours through the sovereign grace of God and not through any merit which we possess.

The Lord Jesus met with His disciples repeatedly before His ascension, and certainly encouraged and authorized such assemblies which in Acts became local churches. John 20:19-29 records two such occasions. They are not here called churches, nor is there yet any indication of the offices of pastor or deacon. But these meetings were not held in synagogues. The brethren assembled were those who were the charter members of the church established in Jerusalem. The Lord did breathe upon them and say, "Receive ye the Holy Ghost" (v. 22). Twice they met thus upon the first day of the week (vv. 19, 26) and experienced the blessed presence of the risen Lord. We certainly see here the superintendence of the Lord Jesus in producing the local church He had promised, even though the final climactic acts of the Spirit's baptism and filling were not experienced until Pentecost. These are transition days at which we are looking, as the Church was produced under the ministry of the Lord Jesus and fully implemented by His gift of the Holy Spirit to guide and comfort (John 16:7).

There can be no adequate comprehension of the Bible unless it is clearly understood that the Church is wholly distinct from Israel. Its origin, nature, conduct and objective are all in contrast to Israel. Much doctrinal error is common today among people failing to recognize this distinction. There are three groups in the world in this age: Jews, Gentiles and the Church of God (1 Cor. 10:32). The first two are unsaved; the last one is saved. When a Jew or a Gentile accepts Christ, he is saved, becomes part of the Church and ceases to be either Jew or Gentile (Gal. 3:28)!

It is a Biblical principle that when more is given, more is required. In view of what the Lord has done for us in this age, therefore, we ought to be more willing than were the saints of past ages to love and praise Him, to serve and sacrifice, to live or die for Him.

The Church Presented

This part of the Church's experience which is still future holds within itself the hush of anticipation in us and, in a sense, in His heart also. All the ages of time have been moving toward this great climax. Christ will perfect the Church and "present it to himself a glorious church, not having spot, or wrinkle, or any such thing . . ." (Eph. 5:27). For this purpose He came and died.

Who can say why an infinite, eternal, self-existent God finds delight in His creatures? We can only rejoice in this fact and delight in the blessed implications it holds for us. This truth, so far beyond our understanding, is stated briefly in Ephesians 1:23 where it speaks of the Church "which is his body, the fulness of him that filleth all in all." As God, of course, He needs nothing to complete Him. But as the "second man" and the "last Adam" (1 Cor. 15:45-47), He humbled Himself and became obedient unto death. Now God has highly exalted Him (Phil. 2:6-11). As the Head of the new creation, He is no more complete without His Bride than Adam would have been without Eve.

Let us consider the preparation for this presentation. On the part of Christ it involves His present work of intercession as our High Priest. He thereby guarantees the safekeeping of those for whom He died as He ever lives to make intercession for us (Heb. 7:25). He, in this ministry, also cleanses and purifies us for that day as He washes us in the water of the Word that we, the Church, might not have "spot, or wrinkle, or any such thing . . ." (Eph. 5:26, 27).

The preparatory work of Christ for that presentation also includes the judgment of believers' works at the Judgment Seat of Christ. We must all appear before that judgment seat as believers (2 Cor. 5:10), not to determine our destiny but to appraise and reveal the quality of our works and service in this life. Read 1 Corinthians 3:11-15. This portion declares that "if any man build upon this foundation [Christ] . . . he himself shall be saved. . . ." Interwoven with that glorious fact is the solemn truth that our works here are to be made manifest at that time. The dross will be consumed, and we shall lose our rewards. All that is for His glory will remain and be rewarded. In that day there will doubtless be real shame and tears for many of us. John warns that we should so live and abide in Him now that "when he shall appear, we may have confidence, and not be ashamed before him at his coming" (1 John 2:28).

This work will certainly precede the presentation of the Church to Christ and the marriage supper of the Lamb. Purification will be complete; reproof will be over; and Glory lies ahead!

On our part, in this age, preparation for that glorious day involves the perfecting of ourselves with the provisions He has given us. The hope of Christ's coming is a purifying power in itself. (See 1 John 3:3.) The prospect of seeing Him should cause us to confess our sins and secure His cleansing (1 John 1:9). We need to be clean.

We are to grow up in Christ as we feed upon His Word (1 Pet. 2:2; Eph. 4:11-32).

We are to be faithful stewards in all things committed to us, including the evangelizing of the world (1 Cor. 4:2).

These and many similar things should enable us to prepare for that day with the care with which a bride prepares for her bridal day. There should be the restraint born of a proper fear of grieving Him and the encouragement of the anticipation of seeing Him and hearing His approval.

When all the preparation of these days is over and the Church is presented to Him, a new ministry will begin. We read in Ephesians 2:7 that in the ages to come He will show the exceeding riches of His grace in His kindness toward us through Christ Jesus. Sinners, transformed by His grace, translated into His presence, will forever vindicate before the whole universe the amazing sacrifice of Christ at Calvary. In that day He will be glorified in His saints and admired in all them that believe (2 Thess. 1:10). In that day "every knee should bow, of things in heaven, and things in earth, and things under the earth; And that every tongue should confess that Jesus Christ is Lord, to the glory of God the Father" (Phil. 2:10, 11). Hallelujah!

2

The Local Church

DID YOU EVER SEE anyone hesitate and frown over the old riddle: "If a lamb's tail is called a leg, how many legs does a lamb have?" Of course the answer is four, since a lamb's tail is not a leg, no matter what it is called! It is equally true that not all organizations are churches that are called by that name. The Word of God has prescribed certain principles that are necessary to constitute a church. In this, as in other things, the imagination of man has departed from the revealed truth because of ignorance of the truth, or in self-will. We purpose, therefore, to examine what the Word says on the vital subject of the church, desiring that, as a result, we shall be able to discern accurately between the true and the false, and thus walk obediently before Him (1 Tim. 3:14, 15).

We need to be honest and ethical in our dealings with other individuals and churches. We must remember, however, that "churches" that are in any of the various cults or modernism or other serious error are not true churches. Actually, they constitute a mission field. People within such groups have a right to hear the truth, and we have a responsibility to give it to them. Probably we have many times been so afraid of being called proselyters that we have avoided dealing with these people. Certainly our basic approach should not be a criticism of their churches, or a mere effort to take them *out* of their group *into* our church. Let us pray for and seek for opportunities to sow the pure seed of the Word in their minds and hearts. If their eyes are opened unto the truth, God will deliver them from error. I do not mean that we should never speak plainly about error; we may need to do so with people involved in it. They need to be warned as well as instructed! We must manifest grace seasoned with salt. People in liberal churches should certainly be led into real New Testament churches when they have accepted Christ.

All men without Christ are perishing, whether in or out of a church. We have a responsibility to preach the Word to every creature and to seek the deliverance of those blinded by the idolatry of modernism (2 Cor. 11:3, 4; Gal. 1:6-9), as well as those blinded by the idolatry of heathenism. Modernism does constitute idolatry in that it preaches "another Jesus." Our Lord Jesus is God manifest in the flesh (1 Tim. 3:16), born of a virgin (Luke 1:35), sinless in all His life (Heb. 7:26), Who died for our sins as our Substitute (1 Cor. 15:3; 2 Cor. 5:21), and arose bodily from the grave (Matt. 28:6; John 20:5-9).

The Jesus preached by the liberals is a great leader, but not God; he was born naturally, out of wedlock; he was great, but he made mistakes; he died only as a martyr; he lives only in a spiritual sense—his body was stolen, not raised from the dead! This is "another Jesus," and to worship him would be as idolatrous as to worship an image of gold, upon which is engraved the name "Jesus." The only difference is that "this Jesus" is made of mental concepts rather than of metal. Neither is God; both are of human origin.

The Lord has given us the apostolic *message* we are to preach. He has also given the apostolic *method* which we are to follow. His method involves the establishment of local churches and the implementation of His work through the church. The liberals have forsaken His message and His method. However, some who preach the gospel have also forsaken His method. Declaring that "the church has failed," they set up other organizations and methods that compete with the churches, and often criticize and oppose them. Money and people are diverted from the churches. Such programs cannot be justified Biblically.

The Origin of a Local Church

We suggest the following brief definition: A local New Testament church is a body of believers immersed upon a credible confession of faith in Jesus Christ, having two officers (pastor and deacons), sovereign in polity, and banded together for work, worship, the observance of the ordinances and the worldwide proclamation of the gospel.

The New Testament clearly indicates that such local churches as this definition outlines came into existence in apostolic times. Churches, basically true to these principles, have doubtless continued down through the ages. As Baptists, however, we do not believe in apostolic succession, or that any such succession is necessary to establish a true church in this day. The possession of apostolic truth is essential to a true church, but that truth is obtained from the Word of

God, and is not necessarily passed as a torch from one church to another, or from one age to another. The New Testament is the charter of the church. It is the law by which it is established and the standard by which it is conducted. If a Bible were dropped into the midst of an otherwise unevangelized tribe, and were read and believed, churches basically like our own would result as men were saved and walked in obedience to the Word. In fact, such cases have been reported by missionaries.

Note in the New Testament that from the beginning of the ministry of the apostles, local churches were established and were the centers of all activity in the Lord's work. Note the references to the church in Jerusalem (Acts 5:11; 8:1; 15:4, 22), in Antioch (Acts 13:1-3), in Judaea, Galilee and Samaria (Acts 9:31), in Syria and Cilicia (Acts 15:41), in Asia (Rev. 1:4), in Thessalonica (1 Thess. 1:1) and many other places. The churches were not only founded but confirmed by careful teaching and apostolic oversight (Acts 16:4, 5). Most of Paul's letters were written to the churches to establish them in the faith.

It is important to observe how consistently the Word describes the local church as the center of missionary work (Acts 13:1-3; 14:23, 27), ministry, fellowship, discipline and all Christian work. We live in a day when this is frequently ignored and even denied. We urge a careful reading of the Book of Acts with this thought in mind. Mark the portions dealing with the churches and their ministry. The principle is clear.

There is an urgent need to establish more New Testament churches in areas without a Biblical ministry. Many churches have assisted believers in neighboring communities in evangelistic meetings, house-to-house visitation and the subsequent organization of a church. More of this could be done. We make the following suggestions briefly to show how simple such an organizational project may be in its details. Once it is prayerfully determined that a church is needed, the following steps are usually taken:

1. A committee of the most capable and consecrated persons available should draw up, or secure, a suitable church covenant, articles of faith and a constitution.

2. Persons interested in membership, but who have letters in other Baptist churches, should secure their letters for the purpose of becoming charter members of this church.

3. A business meeting is then called to consider the covenant, articles of faith and constitution. A series of meetings may be necessary to bring them into final form and adopt them as the expression of the convictions of those forming the church.

4. A motion is then made to organize the church.

5. Officers may then be elected, including the calling of a pastor (who may already be on the field as a missionary).

6. A recognition council may then be called, not to constitute the church, but to seek the counsel, confidence and fellowship of sister churches.

7. It is usually good to proceed with the incorporation of the group to provide certain legal benefits, including the ability to own property.

8. Churches, as well as individuals, need fellowship. It is wise for the church when it is organized to apply for fellowship in an association of churches, such as the General Association of Regular Baptist Churches, and the state and local associations of those churches.

A helpful book on this subject and other related problems is the standard volume on Baptist polity, *The New Directory for Baptist Churches,* by Edward T. Hiscox.

The Membership of a Local Church

The Bible does teach membership in a local church even though this teaching is sometimes denied. This is evident from the direct teaching on discipline, in such terms as: ". . . Put away from among yourselves that wicked person" (1 Cor. 5:13). The church cannot put out one who was not taken in. As Paul declares in the preceding verse, we are to judge those who are within, not those without. Furthermore, churches in New Testament times transacted their business (Acts 15:22). And in order to do so decently and in order, it is logically necessary that a definite, qualified group be determined which can vote on such business.

Qualifications for membership.   Membership qualifications in a local church include salvation, baptism, and sound doctrine and conduct.

Salvation. No one should be brought into the church with an expectancy that simply by being in this atmosphere he may be saved. As Paul wrote to the church at Rome, he addressed the letter, "To all that be in Rome, beloved of God, called to be saints . . ." (1:7); to the Colossians, "To the saints and faithful brethren in Christ which are at Colosse . . ." (1:2). God is a Spirit and requires that we "worship him in spirit and in truth" (John 4:24). That which is born of the flesh is flesh, and we are not spiritual beings until we have been born again (John 3:3-6). Then, and not until then, we "as lively stones, are built up a spiritual house . . ." (1 Pet. 2:5). Churches that are careless regarding this basic principle are soon infiltrated by the unregenerate with their carnal methods and lives. Such a church has lost its power and usefulness, and really ceases to be a Biblical church, regardless of its professed doctrinal position.

Baptism. The apostles knew nothing of unimmersed believers. They who gladly received the Word were baptized (Acts 2:41). See such other instances as Acts 8:35-39 and 16:32-34. Matthew 28:19 and 20 prescribe the order we are to follow: Make disciples, baptize them and teach them to observe all that He commanded. Peter commanded believers to be baptized (Acts 10:47, 48). He did not compel, but he did command. This act is the first step of obedience to our risen Lord. For a believer to neglect or reject immersion is to be disobedient, and while in disobedience he is not ready for church membership. This is not to say that a person must be sinless—in which case there would be no members! It is not a case of Baptists magnifying baptism above all other things. It is a preliminary step of obedience which any babe in Christ can take. No one should be received into membership who is saying, "I will not," to any command of the Word.

Sound doctrine and conduct. While Baptists do not believe the Word teaches a probation period, the person coming into the church should be committed to the truth in faith and conduct, and should subsequently demonstrate reality in both. If after membership is granted, there is serious irregularity which cannot be corrected with patient teaching and prayer, the individual is to be put out of fellowship (see Acts 8:13-24; Rom. 16:17; 2 Thess. 3:6).

It is highly desirable that pastor and deacons carefully examine all persons before recommending them to the church for membership. Many dangers are to be avoided:

1. It is fair to the candidates for membership to know what the church believes and expects, with what group it affiliates, etc. Frank discussion at this point will save many heartaches later.

2. Informal discussion often clarifies the thinking of the immature or the uninstructed, and helps to establish them as fruitful members.

3. Careful examination of the doctrinal position of prospective members may reveal basic errors that make membership unwise until these matters are corrected. It is far better to deal with the problem at this point than to allow it to bring controversy into the church later. No thinking person, worthy of membership, will object to careful examination carried on in a Christlike spirit.

4. Many people seek to join churches with wrong motives. I suggest a few common ones: (1) to provide a respectable front for a worldly life; (2) to secure business advantages; (3) to obtain social opportunities for themselves or their families; (4) to seek an outlet for a desire for leadership or self-exaltation.

5. Some people are chronic troublemakers who move from church to church and bring strife and division to each one. They have fair and flattering speeches about how wonderful this church is compared to the one where they have recently been treated so unfairly! Unusual caution should be exercised before receiving such persons. The pastor of the church they are leaving should be consulted. His side of the story may be very revealing!

6. Well-meaning but dangerous prospective members are those who leave other denominations and seek membership in a Baptist church simply because they like the new preacher and his message of grace. If they see and confess the error of their former connections and grasp clearly the distinctive doctrinal position of Baptists, they usually prove to be most excellent members! But if they do not make a clear break with the old position, they bring that error into the church and cause confusion and division in the years ahead. Many a church has felt flattered by the coming of numbers of such people, only to find later that the church has lost its distinctive, Biblical position because of the aggressive activity of this new group of non-Baptists. The church has become divided with strife because of the members who never really became convinced on the distinctive doctrinal position of the church. Many such people have been in unsound churches. They visit a Baptist church and are thrilled to hear the gospel again. However, before they are received as members, they should also come to believe the other Biblical doctrines. They should be convinced, for instance, that the immersion of a believer is the only mode of scriptural baptism. Many people of this kind will consent to baptism, saying, "I am willing to be immersed." This is not enough! Baptism is not an initiation, nor a price to pay for the privilege of membership. It is a divine command. Withhold membership until the candidate comes by conviction!

Churches are not established for perfect people, or there would be no members! But they are established for God's people who love Him and seek to serve Him and help one another. Church membership rolls should be handled in the light of these facts.

Reception of members.   Members are received into the church by one of four ways.

Baptism. By this is meant that when a believer who is unimmersed asks to be received into the church, the church properly votes to receive the person following his baptism. The membership is not implemented until the baptism is performed.

Letter. One who has been Biblically immersed as a believer, and has joined a New Testament church, may transfer his membership to another church of "like faith and order" by securing a church letter which commends him to the other church specifically, as one who is in good standing in the church issuing the letter. The church into which he comes must, of course, vote to receive him before the transfer is valid. It is under no obligation to receive him. Great care needs to be exercised because, unfortunately, some churches issue letters carelessly to those who are not worthy of commendation. This ought not to be done. The usual practice is not to receive by letter from other than a Baptist church. Those coming from other groups are usually received by baptism or, under some conditions, by experience.

It should be understood that letters are not normally given to individuals. Letters should be sent from one church to another at the request of the individual and upon the vote of the church. The procedure should begin at the church where the prospective member has asked to join. When the letter has been received and the candidate has been taken into the membership, the dismissing church should be notified to prevent dual membership. If for any reason a letter is not requested or received, the church taking the new member should notify the former church to remove the name from its rolls.

Experience. In some cases baptized believers, qualified for membership, are unable to produce a church letter. Their former church may have dissolved. They may have been out of fellowship and been dropped from membership, but are now revived and walking with the Lord. They are received upon the testimony of their experience of salvation and baptism.

Restoration.

Release of members.   Members are released from membership in only four ways.

Letter of dismissal to church of like faith and order by which membership of one in good and regular standing is transferred with commendation.[1]

Letter of dismissal to church not of like faith and order by which a member is dismissed without commendation. This letter is also used for a member who is not in good and regular standing.

Discipline for any cause which justifies the church's terminating the covenant relationship, such as false doctrine or immorality. Any member who has conducted himself in such manner as to merit church discipline may not be dropped from the church rolls at his own request, since such procedure would remove him from the authority of the church.

1. This may also be called a letter of transfer.

Death.

The Lord has graciously designed the local church, and our relationship to it, to provide us a spiritual home for nurture, fellowship, testimony and discipline. He has commanded that we are not to forsake the assembling of ourselves together because He knows our need for this relationship. Church membership is considered a sacred and perpetual obligation, and is not to be terminated as one might drop out of a club. We belong to the Lord forever and have a lifelong obligation and privilege to work and fellowship with His people in a New Testament church until we enter His presence through death.

Inactive membership.   Many churches maintain an inactive membership list. Those on this list were formerly active members. Because of failure to fulfill their Biblical and covenant obligations, they are placed on the inactive list under provisions within the church constitution. This is done by vote of the church upon recommendation of the pastor and deacons. At least once a year the membership list should be reviewed and persons should be removed from active membership if all efforts fail to win them back to walk with the Lord and His people.

While in this inactive status, the member should not be entitled to vote, hold office or teach.

Every effort should be made to reclaim those on the inactive list, but if these endeavors fail, after one year they should be dropped from the membership.

When there is satisfactory evidence of a renewed spiritual walk on the part of any member on the inactive list, he should be restored to active membership by vote of the church upon recommendation of the pastor and deacons.

Associate membership.   Some churches have adopted a classification called associate membership. This is very uncommon among Baptists and is not recommended. If it is used to accommodate those who are not immersed, or who differ on some doctrinal positions, it is dangerous and unbiblical.

There is no indication in the Word that the apostles or apostolic churches temporized with unbelief or disobedience. On the contrary, the Scriptures declare: ''Then they that gladly received his word were baptized: and the same day there were added unto them about three thousand souls. And they continued stedfastly in the apostles' doctrine and fellowship, and in breaking of bread, and in prayers'' (Acts 2:41, 42).

If associate membership is used only for those who are fully qualified as active members, but who wish to retain their membership in another church, it still is undesirable. This classification is sometimes used for students who are away from their hometown and church. However, church membership involves certain covenant relationships which make it impossible to belong to two churches simultaneously. It is best to move the church letter to the new residence if there is a sound church with which to affiliate. This is the covenant agreement.

For additional information, see chapter 8 and Appendix A (the suggested form for "Letter of Watchcare").

3

The Government
of the Church

THE FORM OF CHURCH government is tremendously important for both the harmony and the permanency of the church and its testimony. Both Scripture and history teach us the need of some duly recognized form of government within the church in order that decisions may be made and business transacted decently and in order.

Scripture and history also witness to the dangers of centralized authority that exalts individuals into a place of power. Such government results in the grossly unbiblical division between the clergy and laity, and subjects the people to a few ecclesiastical leaders in a way that God never intended. It is widely believed to be this error of which the Lord declared: ". . . Which thing I hate" (Rev. 2:15).

In view of satanic strategy, the more centralized the church authority, the greater is the danger. It is vastly easier and quicker to capture the thinking and cooperation of a few men than that of a multitude. Therefore, the denominations which vested in a few the power to direct and determine the actions and policies, and to make the decisions, were more vulnerable to satanic attack. By capturing the leadership, the entire denomination became corrupted. Greater speed and efficiency may be acquired by concentrating authority, providing that those with the power are both capable and honest. But the danger is too great because of the greed and selfishness of the human heart. Not only does God warn about these things, but history demonstrates that centralized organizations have been turned to liberalism and unbelief more quickly than others. Baptists have resisted this trend longer than most, partly for this reason.

Simplicity

We live in an age when the Lord is dealing directly with individual men, through the ministry of the Holy Spirit, without the intervention of any priesthood—that of the Old Testament or any other. He established the Church in which all believers are priests to stand before Him as the sons of our Aaron, the Lord Jesus Christ (1 Pet. 2:9; Rev. 1:6). With wonderful simplicity, without formalism or ritualism, we may approach Him in the true holy place (Heb. 10:19-22). This same simplicity marks our ministry to men as we proclaim Christ our Savior to the multitudes of this world (2 Cor. 5:20, 21).

The government of the local churches is equally direct and uninvolved. There were no "wheels within wheels" in the conduct of the Lord's work in the New Testament times. These things have come upon us through the schemes of men. Brethren in Christ met together to worship Him, preach His Word and administer His work. There was no evidence of any authority external to the local church. In that day, before the New Testament was written, the Lord provided apostles to speak with authority in the instruction of the churches, to the extent that Paul wrote: ". . . Hold the traditions which ye have been taught, whether by word, or our epistle" (2 Thess. 2:15). However, with the completing of the canon of Scripture and the termination of the gift of apostles, no other such power remains; all instruction comes to us from the Lord through His Word.

The centralizing influence of the convention system among the Baptists has been one of the entering wedges of liberalism. The Lord never intended churches to be other than local, sovereign units, responsible directly to Him. Voluntary cooperation with one another is scriptural (2 Cor. 8:18-23), but the centralizing of finances and authority immediately exposes the churches to more dangers. The autonomous local church has the protection from ecclesiastical overlordship, but enjoys the benefits of centralized authority if she is subject to her Head, the Lord Jesus Christ, Who is infinitely capable and righteous!

Four forms of government are typical within Christendom.

Papal.   This, of course, is seen in the Roman Catholic Church, more recently and more accurately called by some the Marian Church. The dangers and the damage of this system are evident to all who have eyes to see. It is utterly without support in the Word of God.

Episcopalian.   Here the authority resides in bishops and other offices of the clergy. This, too, is without scriptural foundation.

Presbyterian.   This is a representative form of government that places authority in sessions, presbyteries, synods and assemblies, rather than in the local church. It cannot be defended from the Word of God.

Congregational.   Here the authority remains with the local church. Individuals or committees may be designated to perform certain responsibilities, but they are directly answerable to the church and to the Lord, Who is the Head of the church. No other center of power or authority is recognized. Baptists have always believed that this is the New Testament pattern of church government. The advent of the convention system violated these Biblical principles.

Baptists believe in democratic procedures that permit open discussion of problems and divergent views. This is right and it is Biblical. Please read carefully Acts 15. Note that this is not a council as is often stated, but a business meeting of the local church in Jerusalem (v. 22). It has many features that we can observe with profit.

This meeting was called to discuss a vital question of doctrine raised by the churches in Antioch, Syria and Cilicia: Must a believer also keep the law in order to be saved? Messengers were sent to secure information as to the doctrine originally sent out by the Lord through the saints at Jerusalem. There is no indication that the Jerusalem church ruled over the other churches, but only that they determined the pure doctrine which they had received, and then verified it to these inquiring churches.

The conduct of the meeting is interesting. Acts 15, for all practical purposes, contains the minutes of that church meeting. The question was freely discussed by many in this big assembly (v. 7), described as a multitude (v. 12). Peter, Barnabas and Paul concluded the discussion. When no one else had anything to add (vv. 12, 13), James, who was obviously the moderator, summarized the discussion and stated the conclusion which had been reached by "the whole church" (vv. 13-22). Although there had been much disputing or discussion (v. 7), the people became quiet and listened attentively (v. 12). The verdict which they reached was a unanimous decision (vv. 22, 25, 28). After the business was cared for, the meeting was adjourned (v. 30). Special messengers, chosen by the church, carried the decision of the meeting to the brethren in Antioch, Syria and Cilicia, in response to their request for information.

This chapter in Acts should encourage us in our churches to participate in free discussions in a prayerful effort to reach unanimous decisions. The expression of personal convictions should never be viewed as carnal controversy, unless the speakers manifest such a spirit, and this is to be avoided! Baptist churches historically have been ruled by congregational vote. We must maintain this Biblical practice and not fall into Presbyterianism, allowing a rule by pastor and deacons. Individual participation is Biblical in both the ministry and the government of a local church.

Thank God for the freedom and sovereignty of our churches! We must guard these privileges against centralization of power within our churches as well as from overlordship from the outside.

In chapter 4 consideration is given to the authority of the pastor within the church.

Independency

We begin this section with a warning. By independency we do not mean isolation, self-sufficiency or self-will.

We may isolate ourselves from our sister churches and rob each other of the blessings of fellowship and the advantages of a concerted testimony. This is not good. However, the measure of that cooperation must be determined by each church for itself, and not be thrust upon it from those on the outside.

We may become self-willed in our attitude, thinking we are responsible to no one, failing to remember that the Lord is the Head of the church. We must give unqualified obedience to Him. Independency is not lawlessness nor irresponsibility. We are our brother's keeper in a real sense, and our independence is qualified by his need.

Independent of the state.   We note that the church is independent of the state. Baptists have always contended for this Biblical principle. It will help to remember that the Lord established three great institutions: *the home, the government* and *the church*. We have responsibilities toward each one, and there is an interdependency in their relationship with each other. Yet each one is sovereign in its own field. Christians are to *obey* civil rulers (Rom. 13), recognizing that the Lord ordained government and granted to men the ultimate authority of capital punishment (Gen. 9:6; Rom. 13:4). We are also to *pray* for civil rulers (1 Tim. 2:1, 2); and we are to *pay* our taxes (Matt. 22:21; Rom. 13:6, 7). The church, in turn, has a right to the protection of civil law as the government deals with evildoers. However, the church has no instructions concerning the administration of civil affairs, nor does the Word ever permit the state to interfere in the conduct of spiritual things.

In defense of this principle, we deny that the Roman Church, Baptists or any other group has any right to federal or state funds to conduct schools or run school buses! There are tax-supported schools to which the children may go at state expense. If any church wishes to conduct its own, it may do so at its own expense; but it may not charge the state without violation of this basic principle, the separation of church and state. We are thankful that many churches now support this doctrine, but even in the early days of our own country few except Baptists did so.

Independent of ecclesiastical authority.   The church is independent of all ecclesiastical authority outside its own membership. The Word of God knows nothing of a centralized church government, convention head-quarters, unified budgets and all the control over local churches which marks such a movement. Baptists have held to this position throughout their history until the recent decadence marked by apostasy, denominational machines and the ecumenical church.

Other denominations consider the entire organization to be a unit and, therefore, speak of themselves as such: the Roman Catholic Church, or the United Presbyterian Church in the U.S.A., etc. But the people denominated as Baptists never describe themselves, or consider themselves, as *the* Baptist Church, but rather as Baptist churches. Incidentally, there are more than twenty-six million Baptists in the United States in the various associations and conventions—the largest non-Catholic group. Methodists are second with nearly thirteen million.[1] Tragically, many who are called Baptists actually have no right to this name because they deny the New Testament revelation.

Historians agree in their declarations concerning the independence of local churches in the first and second centuries. The following quotations are characteristic:

Mosheim (Lutheran): "During a great part of this [second] century all the churches continued to be, as at first, independent of each other. Each church was a kind of small, independent republic, governing itself by its own laws, enacted or at least sanctioned by the people."

Waddington (Episcopal): "It is also true that in the earliest government of the first Christian society, that of Jerusalem, not the elders only, but the whole church, were associated with the apostles."

Coleman (Congregational): "These churches, wherever formed, became separate and independent bodies, competent to appoint their officers and administer their own government without reference or subordination to any central authority or foreign power. No fact connected with the history of the primitive churches is more fully established or more generally conceded."

We suggest this historical evidence only to indicate that the early Christians obviously understood the Scriptures on this subject just as we do today. Our final authority is the Word of God, and we present two portions of Scripture as clear examples of the independence of the local church.

In Matthew 18:15-17 the Lord gave instructions as to the settlement of controversies between members of a local church. The proce-

---

1. Statistics from *Yearbook of American and Canadian Churches, 1978.*

dure is clear and well-known, but is very seldom practiced! First, the differences are to be resolved between the individuals if possible, with the offended brother making the first effort toward reconciliation. Second, if the offender will not be reconciled, there is to be a second attempt by the offended, this time with one or two witnesses. Third, if he will not hear them, then "tell it unto the church. . . ." Fourth, "if he neglect to hear the church"—this is the crux of the whole argument that we want to be clear—*if he will not hear the church, what is the next court of appeal?* Is it the bishop, the conference or the synod? *Nothing is higher but God!* If he will not hear the church, he is to be "unto thee as an heathen man and a publican." That is, he is to be refused fellowship by the action of the church until he demonstrates the reality of his faith by the acknowledgment of his sin. Then he is again to be restored, as taught elsewhere.

It appears, therefore, that in the matter of discipline no authority is higher than the local church. (See also 1 Corinthians 5.)

Again, in Acts 15 we have the inspired account of the settlement of a very crucial doctrinal matter. A local church was the final court of appeal. It was determined that Paul, Barnabas and some others go to Jerusalem to consult with the apostles and elders.

It is interesting to note that the church paid their way (v. 3), and that they were received in Jerusalem by the *church,* as well as by the apostles and elders (v. 4).

Beginning with verse 6 and continuing through verse 29, we have a record of the business meeting of the church in Jerusalem where this vital question was considered and settled. Note that apart from the brethren who came seeking the solution, no one was there but those affiliated with this church. The apostles were unquestionably members there. They even remained in the city during the heat of the persecution (Acts 8:1). Jerusalem was their home. The elders were pastors in this very large church (Acts 4:4; 5:14). This doctrinal difference was not settled in a committee room nor by apostolic authority alone. This was a meeting of the congregation (15:22).

Dependency

While the church is independent of outside organizations and authority, there is a vital internal dependency.

In the interest of efficient operation, a church may well authorize and foster organizations within itself, such as a Sunday school, youth groups and a missionary society. Several well-defined principles should be observed, however, concerning the dependency of these groups upon the will of the church. Often they are allowed to become independent organizations, competing with the church for loyalty and support.

We suggest the following principles to protect the church against abuses that often are suffered from improper administration of internal organizations. There may be some justifiable modifications under some local conditions.

1. Officers of these organizations are subject to church approval and may be removed by the church.

2. All officers, leaders and teachers in such groups should be members of the local church and in happy accord with its doctrine and practice.

3. The standards and policies of these groups should be subject to the approval of the church.

4. Whenever possible, it is well to combine the funds of the internal groups in the common treasury under the church treasurer. These funds are then included in the report of the treasurer, showing the receipts, disbursements and balance of each group, and are also included in the audit of church funds.

5. Reports from each of the organizations should be given in the business meetings of the church.

6. All organizations should seek the counsel of the pastor and be open to receive his leadership and suggestions.

7. The members of these organizations, while seeking to win the lost and to bring them into their classes and groups, should have a major concern to bring these souls into the relationship of membership in the church itself.

Since the local church is the only administrative authority which the Lord has established, the individual Christian should recognize his responsibility toward his church, its program, decisions, needs, members and pastor.

4

Who Controls the Church?

IN PRACTICE there is a wide diversity of answers to the question, Who controls the local church? Since the Lord established the church, He must have a plan, and the only place where we can find His revealed will is the Word of God. Unfortunately, we are too prone to inject our own thinking as authoritative. Our varied denominational backgrounds, and our training or lack of training, often affect our viewpoints more than actual searching of the Word of God.

Much trouble has come into churches because of faulty answers to the above question. May the Lord enable us to walk Biblically in this vital matter. Here are a few pertinent points for consideration:

The Head of the Church

Christ is "the head over all things to the church, Which is his body . . ." (Eph. 1:22, 23). Unless the head directs the body, the body acts erratically. When the head controls each part of the body individually, there is perfect coordination between the members. This should be true in the local church, which is the local manifestation of His Body. Then the members "have the same care for another" (see 1 Cor. 12:12-31). When there is strife in a local church, it is evident that some, if not all, of the members are not submissive to the Head.

The Pastor

The pastor is the shepherd and the bishop or overseer of the flock. (See Acts 20:17-28 and 1 Peter 5:1-4.) Hebrews 13 certainly speaks of the bishops or pastors when it says, "Obey them that have the rule over you, and submit yourselves: for they watch for your souls . . ." (v. 17).

The pastor is not the hired man of the church, subject to all the whims of the members. He is God's prophet. As he faithfully serves the Lord and preaches the Word, he is to be counted worthy of double honor (1 Tim. 5:17; 1 Thess. 5:12, 13). An elder, or pastor, is not to be rebuked (1 Tim. 5:1) unless he is known to be walking in sin (5:20). No accusation is to be received against him unless there is adequate testimony to its accuracy (5:19). However, there is no justifiable basis for a pastor to seek to escape the consequence of sin by crying, "Touch not mine anointed . . ." (1 Chron. 16:22).

His authority in the church, as God's leader, is a moral and spiritual power, not a legal one. He should exercise leadership. He must refuse to compromise Biblical convictions, even though he should be gracious in attitude, and never be stubborn about personal opinions or desires that do not involve Biblical principles. His authority rests in the power of a godly example, as well as in the fact that he is a Biblical officer (1 Pet. 5:3; Eph. 4:11, 12). However, he is not to be a lord "over God's heritage" (1 Pet. 5:1-4). He has no Biblical right to be autocratic, dictatorial or domineering. No man of God, filled with the Spirit, will manifest such an attitude.

The Deacons

The deacons are also Biblically provided officers within the church. Their qualifications are outlined in 1 Timothy 3, following those of the bishop or pastor. Almost certainly they first appear in Scripture in Acts 6:1-8. They are to be godly men, full of the Holy Spirit.

The word *deacon* means "servant." These officers are the servants of the Lord and of the church. They are invaluable helpers with the pastors. Unfortunately, some deacon boards conceive of themselves to be a board of directors in charge of the corporation, and feel that under their direction the pastor, and even the people, must move in full obedience. Nothing could be farther from the New Testament position. Many churches have been torn apart because some deacon, or deacons, misunderstood the divine order in this matter, and became dictatorial, assuming authority the Lord never gave.

The Church

The church is a group ruled by its own majority vote. Neither the pastor nor the deacons can rule the church. This is clear from Matthew 18:17 where the church is the final authority in discipline. It is also evident from Acts 15 where the whole church determined the vital decision on true doctrine. The church has divinely provided officers and' leaders, but the Lord has chosen to rest the final power in the entire group, subject to His own Headship.

The Divine Design

It is evident, therefore, that the Lord has designed the church with internal, interlocking powers and responsibilities. The church is to be subject to the pastor. Yet the pastor is subject to the church, in another sense, for he is called by them and may be disciplined by them.

There is no problem here except for those who will not be subject to the Head of the church. It is not difficult for a Bible-taught church to be subject to the overseer or pastor that God has sent. Neither is it difficult for a faithful pastor to be sensitive to the will of God's people. What a lovely and delightful relationship exists between pastor, deacons and people when all are subject to Christ the Head.

It is vital that this happy relationship should always be evident in each church. When there is jealousy, bitterness, self-seeking and strife, the testimony of the Lord suffers, saints and sinners are caused to stumble, and the church loses its power to be a blessing because the Holy Spirit is grieved. Pastor and people must both recognize that the honor of the Lord and the welfare of His church must take precedence over personal differences. Let us suffer wrong. Let us "lose face." But the Lord must not be dishonored, His church be divided, or sinners be offended.

5

The Officers
of the Church

SINCE THE CHURCH is a divine institution, every aspect of its administration is important, including proper, scriptural officers. There is a wide variety of practice in various denominations, varying from the Roman Church with nearly a dozen divisions of the clergy, to the simple Biblical mode of pastors and deacons as practiced by Baptists.

Much of the diversity results from ignoring the Word and developing an organization on the basis of expediency. Some difference results, however, from misunderstanding concerning the titles used in Scripture. We shall try to outline briefly the teaching of the Bible, as we are convinced it is given, in order that the subsequent points will be more clear. Very honest differences of opinion may exist unless it is understood that the terms *pastor, elder* and *bishop* refer to the same office. We shall give three portions of the Word that establish this point:

In 1 Peter 5:1-4 the pastor is discussed. He is the shepherd who is to feed the flock of God. In this portion the pastor is called an elder *(presbuteros)* in verse 1; and is charged in verse 2 with the "oversight," which is from the Greek word that is usually translated "bishop" *(episcopos)*.

In Titus 1:5-7 the terms are again applied to the same person, as Paul writes: ". . . Ordain elders in every city. . . . For a bishop must be blameless. . . ."

In Acts 20:17-28 Paul calls the elders of the church at Ephesus to talk with them. In the final verse he calls these elders "overseers" (that is, bishops, *presbuteros*). He charges these bishops, or elders, to do the work of the pastor or shepherd: "Take heed . . . to all the flock . . . to feed the church of God. . . ."

"Elder" indicates the dignity of the office and "bishop," the duties. "Pastor" gives the relationship to the flock. "Minister" is sometimes applied also *(diakonos)* as one who serves others, signifying the proper attitude of humility. But it is all one office, now commonly called that of the pastor.

Pastors

Qualifications of the pastor.   These are outlined in 1 Timothy 3:1-7. These standards should be considered carefully by a church before calling a man. Godliness of life is the basic element. It is to be feared that sometimes we are too much influenced by glamor and a glib tongue. The qualifications extend into the faithfulness of his ministry. He is to be "apt to teach" (1 Tim. 3:2; 2 Tim. 2:24). He is to preach the Word with urgency and to "reprove, rebuke, exhort with all longsuffering and doctrine" (2 Tim. 4:2). Pastors may or may not be gifted orators, but they must give to the flock the whole counsel of God. This will not always be a pleasing ministry. There is a time to rebuke sin. No man is qualified to be a pastor who is more concerned with pleasing men than pleasing God. Beware of such men.

Good judgment, leadership ability, financial integrity, a life of prayer and a well-ordered family are practical aspects of his life that should adorn the sound doctrine which he preaches.

Some years ago a leader in another denomination declared that in all the years in which churches had sought his help in finding pastors, he had received many requests for well-educated men, or good mixers, or good musicians, but no one had ever said, "Send us a man of God!" May we never forget that above all other characteristics, a pastor must be a man of God!

Calling a pastor.   Calling a pastor is a critical time for the church and should be marked with earnest prayer by the whole church. Chapter 6 deals with this important matter more thoroughly.

Ordination.   Ordination constitutes a public recognition, on the part of the ordaining church, of the man's call and qualifications as a servant of the Lord. Chapter 16 provides additional information on this.

Church's responsibility to the pastor.   This must be guarded carefully if there is to be a mutually happy relationship. Rebellion against constituted authority marks this age. It is evident in all departments of life: politics, economics, literature, art, music, etc. This spirit has also permeated many churches with tragic results. In its ultimate form, it has caused the rejection of the Word of God and its authority. In less intense form, it has resulted in the rejection of the Biblical leadership of the pastor and has injected strife and rebellion against the Biblical standards of the church. Obviously, this is of the enemy, and it has greatly hindered the work of the Lord.

We who profess to love and serve the Lord must carefully avoid this sin of lawlessness. With that objective in view, let us consider some thoughts on the attitudes and responsibilities of the church to its pastor.

Pastors are the Biblical bishops or overseers of the church. They are to be counted worthy of double honor, especially those who labor in the Word (1 Tim. 5:17). Pastors do not always have personalities pleasing to us, nor do they do their work in ways which we prefer. However, we are admonished to "esteem them very highly in love for their *work's* sake" (1 Thess. 5:13). The office and the work of God's servants command our esteem, even when personal fancies are not favorable. We suggest several practical ways to implement a correct attitude of the church toward its pastor.

1. The pastor should be treated with respect. He should not be addressed by his first name, especially in public or before young people. The dignity of the office must be sustained in such ways as this.

2. A pastor is not immune to censure and discipline if he is unsound in doctrine or life. But he must be dealt with very carefully lest we disrupt the work of the Lord and lest we deal falsely with the servant of the Lord. Charges against him are not to be received lightly (1 Tim. 5:19). If he is guilty, he is to be dealt with (v. 20).

However, a pastor must not be the object of gossip and careless criticism. Many families that deal critically with the pastor and his message at the Sunday dinner table wonder tearfully why their children and young people are not more interested in the pastor's ministry and in the Lord and His people! Many wives pray earnestly for unsaved husbands; yet they openly criticize the pastor and review the gossip about the church in the presence of their husbands.

We are to go to the pastor first if we have anything against him. If we are spiritual and he is wrong, this is the Biblical order (Gal. 6:1). If we are carnal and cannot go to him, then we have no right to condemn him! We need first to cast the beam out of our own eyes (Matt. 7:5). Failure to clarify a serious matter with the pastor after prayerful effort may make it advisable to discuss the problem with the deacons.

3. The pastor must not be ignored or bypassed in favor of a former pastor. When a man leaves the pastorate of a church, he is no longer the pastor of that church. No man who is wise and ethical will continue

to counsel and to intervene in the affairs of his former church, and members of that church should not embarrass him with requests to do so. This is divisive.

This principle applies generally to the practice of a man returning to a former church for weddings, funerals and the like. Sometimes, with the wholehearted consent of the pastor, such an arrangement may be made without creating problems. But this is definitely the exception. Even in this situation, the present pastor should have a major part in the joint service.

4. The pastor is a busy man. He must give much time to study and to prayer. He is responsible for much correspondence and office work. There are committees and endless details. He has many hospital calls and needs to spend much time in visitation of new people, as well as in helping the members spiritually. Soul winning is a major responsibility. Many hours are spent in counseling. He must spend adequate time with his own family.

Never impose needlessly upon his time—on the phone, at the office or in the home. Respect his morning in the study and his days off. He must accomplish his work, and he must also have time to relax. Few people realize the drain on a pastor's strength as he gives himself in empathy to those who sorrow or are burdened or perplexed. Pray for him, and do everything possible to help him and lighten his load.

5. While pastors certainly must avoid covetousness as a sin, churches are responsible to care adequately for the material needs of the pastor. Many times he will need an income above the average of the congregation. Few people realize the extensive expense to which he is subjected. Abnormal amounts of travel (usually in behalf of members of the church), extra clothing because of the nature of his work, unusual amounts of entertaining and similar expenses, and the purchase of a suitable library make a substantial income necessary to enable him to carry on his work effectively.

A church that is penurious with a pastor violates the Scripture. Rarely does such a church manifest spiritual power or progress. The principles revealed in 2 Corinthians 9:6-10 are worthy of consideration.

The Scripture makes clear that the laborer is worthy of his hire (Luke 10:7), and that we are to minister in carnal things to those who minister to us in spiritual things (1 Cor. 9:11). The salary should be reviewed by the deacons or the advisory board at least annually. Raises in the salary to help and to encourage the pastor should be granted from year to year under normal circumstances. If this is not done, especially during times of rising living costs, the pastor actually receives a salary cut year after year.

Our pastors will be better pastors if we remember these principles. We should pray for them, honor them, esteem them, give to them and obey them (Heb. 13:16-18).

Pastor's responsibility to the church.   This concern is equally vital. We outline a few of these areas.

1. Diligent, faithful application to his work. This includes much study of the Word—that he may grow and that he may be able to feed the flock with a rich, Biblical ministry. It also includes much activity in visitation and counseling. The office responsibilities in correspondence and similar duties are to be cared for promptly. (A pastor may need secretarial help or other assistance, depending upon the size of the church and other factors.)

2. Proper organization and scheduling of his work. In this he needs the cooperation of the church.

3. Maintaining a sound financial reputation in the paying of bills and wise management of his home, family, car, etc.

4. Proper appearance and social conduct, including suitable attire, poise and conversation.

5. Maintaining a reputation of being upright and ethical. He must tell the truth at all times. He must avoid all appearance of evil. He must never become involved in any irregularity of moral conduct. He must not gossip. There must be no jealousy of others, including fellow pastors who may be prospering more than he. He should carefully avoid critical, premature judgment of others, including fellow pastors. He must not proselyte or seek to advance himself or his church at the expense of other Bible-preaching pastors and churches.

He should not candidate in any church unless he is honestly seeking the Lord's will and is open to consider prayerfully a call from that church. Careless, selfish or proud motives have prompted some men to candidate when they know that a call will not be accepted. This is most unfair to a church and results in much unnecessary discouragement for them. Such practices also ruin the reputation of the pastor.

Frankness and honesty are vital when candidating. A man should never hide his convictions in an effort to secure a call. On the contrary, to avoid future misunderstandings, he will be wise if he submits in writing to the pulpit committee any known areas of divergence from the church in matters of doctrine or practice.

Deacons

Qualifications of deacons.   These are found in 1 Timothy 3:8-13. If Acts

6:1-8 discusses the appointment of the first deacons, as many believe, additional information is given in that portion. These men are to be full of the Holy Ghost and wisdom. They are to be mature leaders, proved in their Christian character in the home, the church and the community.

The title "deacon" *(diakonos)* means a minister or a servant of others. This word is applied to the Lord Himself, that He "came not to be ministered unto, but to minister, and to give his life a ransom for many" (Matt. 20:28). The word here seems to be used to describe the humility of His ministry rather than any office. But the term is used in a specific sense in 1 Timothy 3, as a title to an office. Certainly, however, it is legitimate to understand that the office should be marked by humble service on the part of the one who fills it. This is, therefore, another basic qualification.

Selection of deacons.   This is the responsibility of the local church, according to Acts 6: ". . . Look ye out among you . . ." (v. 3). The qualifications are also given in 1 Timothy that they might know how to conduct themselves "in the house of God, which is the church of the living God . . ." (3:14, 15).

Since no specific method is outlined, the church is allowed to use its prayerful judgment and experience. Church constitutions usually state these conclusions in order that the business may be carried on in an orderly way. Deacons may be elected by a majority vote of the church, or by a two-thirds or a three-fourths majority, whichever the church determines. Such voting should be by ballot. Serious, prayerful consideration should be given to this selection well in advance. First Timothy should be pondered, and its commands and standards observed in the decision. No man should be given this sacred responsibility on the basis of personal friendship. If no qualified men are available, it is better for the office to be vacant temporarily than to fill it with carnal men, or novices, who may greatly damage the testimony and be further hindered by pride in their own lives. Churches will do well to heed these words of admonition.

Term of office.   This varies, depending upon the judgment of the church. The Scripture is silent on this matter. Some churches ordain deacons for life, but this is becoming very rare. Probably the average church elects for a three-year term, reelecting as often as desired. This is a wholesome situation, permitting the church to rotate this office within its membership as much as desired or to retain the leadership of some experienced men as long as needed. Since this is a board of local members, it does not afford the problem that would be posed by calling a pastor to a church as a shepherd for a limited term only.

Duties of deacons.   Their duties are indicated by their name, "servants," and by their relationship to the pastor as described in 1 Timothy 3—the second officers or assistants to the pastor. Furthermore, Acts 6 indicates that while they cared for the temporal needs of the poor within the church, they also carried on a spiritual ministry as men full of the Holy Ghost. Stephen is a great challenge to all our deacons to mingle a flaming testimony for Christ with the more drab and routine duties which are also theirs. May they be constantly reminded of the example set by the life of this godly man. And may they, by the grace of God, emulate it.

Trustees and Other Officers

Trustees are required by law if a church is incorporated. The church has a sovereign right to appoint such officers as are needed, including also treasurer, clerk and others.

Trustees are usually elected as a separate board, parallel to the deacons, and charged with the care of the property. No double standard of life should be allowed as has sometimes been done. All church officers should be spiritual leaders—not merely men with a keen business ability. We need gifted leaders who are also filled with the Holy Spirit.

An increasing number of churches are electing only one "board" and thus designate the deacons as the trustees. This has the disadvantage of not spreading leadership responsibility as widely as possible. This may be overcome by enlarging the number of deacons if qualified men are available. The "single board" plan may develop more efficient operation. Responsibilities do not fall between the groups by misunderstanding. Some very unfortuante—and unnecessary—jealousies may be eliminated. It will also prevent a dual spiritual standard for the two offices.

6

Calling the Pastor

THE CALLING OF A PASTOR is one of the most crucial actions of a church. A pastor's influence for good or evil is tremendous. It is vital that the church secure God's man for this position, or the progress of many years may be lost, and heartaches for the future may be multiplied.

Unfortunately many churches face this significant decision woefully unprepared. Often the members have never been instructed on how to proceed in calling a pastor, and they have had no experience in many years. Sometimes the committee is composed of persons who have been saved recently, or who have been saved out of other denominational backgrounds and have no knowledge of how a Baptist church conducts its business. Still worse, it may be that members of the pulpit committee are not friendly toward the Baptist position and are prejudiced in favor of interdenominational men.

Other dangers confront a church at such a time, no matter how sincerely the members want the Lord's will.

Unworthy Men

Many men who seek pastorates are unqualified or unworthy for such ministry, and no one should be called who has not been thoroughly investigated. Men with any of the following characteristics should be avoided:

1. Those too lazy to work.
2. Those too contentious to cooperate successfully with other people.
3. Those too weak and vacillating to provide sound leadership.
4. Those who are unable to manage their own finances and who are, therefore, in perpetual financial distress.

5. Those who are not morally sound.

6. Those whose families are rebellious and undisciplined (1 Tim. 3:1-7).

7. Those who are opportunists, willing to talk like Baptists when there is an open pulpit, but who have no such convictions and have not lived and preached such a Biblical position.

8. Those who are not in real doctrinal harmony with the position of the church.

9. Those who may be Baptists, but who are in sympathy with other associations and will lead the church away from its present connections to another fellowship. (Such men have a right to their own convictions, but they are very unethical if they accept a church pretending to be in harmony, and then steal the church.)

10. Those who are inadequately prepared for such a ministry.

It is not enough to ask the candidate general questions on these matters. His past record should be checked and detailed questions asked. No man worthy of such a position would object to a thorough investigation.

A Pattern of Procedure

While there is good evidence that the apostolic churches selected their own pastors, no specific pattern of procedure is outlined in the Bible. However, the following suggestions are within the scope of Biblical principles and are founded upon the experience of churches throughout the past years.

1. Many churches have found it wise to have a permanent pulpit committee, consisting of the deacons and some other mature, spiritual members elected by the church. This committee can be given some experience helpful for future responsibilities if the pastor will consult the committee in the choice of pulpit supplies, evangelists, Bible teachers and other special speakers. The members of this committee should be godly, praying people, in full accord with the Biblical position of the church.

2. A pastor may be of great help to his church by teaching the members how to call a pastor long before he even considers resigning.

3. After a pastor has resigned, the pulpit committee should meet for prayer and planning. Many meetings should be held to face and solve the problem confronting them: Who is God's man for this place? The committee should welcome suggestions from members of the church. They may well consult some other trusted pastors for suggestions and guidance. They are wise to seek recommendations from

sound Baptist schools and from some of the Association leaders. Unfortunately, the committee can expect to receive a considerable number of "applications" from men "seeking a job." These should be screened carefully, for the list will probably include men who are not wanted elsewhere for a good reason.

4. The pulpit committee has doubtless given consideration to the type of pastor needed at this time. Some men have special gifts as teachers, personal workers or evangelists. Others have abilities in developing needed organization within the church, or in leadership in building campaigns. A consideration of the local needs, and of the men recommended, may raise a vital interest in one of more of these men. Further inquiries about these few may center the interest and give some indication of the Lord's direction in the matter.

5. At this point, the committee may well go and visit the church of the man about whom they are concerned. This should be unannounced to the man in order that he may be seen and heard in his natural ministry. (It may save fruitless travel to determine beforehand whether the man is to be in his pulpit on the chosen date.) If the committee is interested, it may quietly arrange a conference with the pastor.

6. If there is a strong sense of interest in the man and a conviction in the committee that he may be God's man for them, the committee should arrange to sit down with him and question him thoroughly as to his doctrinal convictions, his convictions on ecclesiastical separation, his financial involvements, his family, his training, his previous experience, his soul winning, his missionary emphasis. Salary, vacations and other matters may be discussed. Beware of cautious, evasive answers. Men who say, "Yes, I can work with your Association," usually mean, but do not say, that they could also work equally well with other groups with widely varying convictions! "Yes, I am a Baptist, but . . ." usually means that the man is an interdenominationalist who would like the prestige and opportunity of a Baptist pulpit.

7. The church may now wish to invite the prospective candidate for a Sunday or, preferably, for a week of meetings or a three-day conference. The members can hear him more frequently, and he can be invited into several homes to develop a closer acquaintance.

8. The pulpit committee may now be sufficiently convinced of the Lord's will to make a unanimous recommendation to the church to call the man as its pastor. When this recommendation is made, a date should be determined according to the church constitution and a business meeting called for an official vote of the church. Most churches require at least a 66-2/3 percent vote for a call. Many require 75 percent, some 90 percent.

9. Whether or not the man is called, he should be informed promptly of the church's decision.

10. Voting on one man at a time has been found a great advantage. Voting on two or more men simultaneously has often resulted in a divided church.

11. Throughout the period, the pulpit committee, as far as possible, should keep the church informed of progress being made. An informed church is more likely to pray, and an uninformed church to gossip and criticize.

12. The committee must be very careful to avoid even the appearance of trying to railroad some man into the church. It must also refuse to yield to personal desires, personal friends or pressure groups that may appear. This work must be a sincere, prayerful effort to find a real man of God who can effectively minister the Word of God and pastor the flock of God.

13. If the church vote does not result in a call, or if the man refuses to accept the call, the committee must continue its work in search of another man.

14. When a pastor is called, it should be for an indefinite time rather than for a year. An annual call has little advantage but many disadvantages. Some churches have decided to vote each year on the pastor after some man overstayed his welcome. Actually, no more damage is done if a church votes to ask for the resignation of an undesirable pastor than is done by refusing to renew the call at the end of the year. In either event, the man is dismissed. (It is, of course, far happier for both parties if a resignation is submitted by mutual consent, if such is needed.) The annual call makes it presumptuous for a pastor to plan his work well in advance and arrange for evangelists, Bible teachers and missionary conferences. It also affords perennial encouragement to troublesome minorities who vex both the pastor and the church.

15. When the pastor and his family arrive, they should be welcomed cordially. Many churches plan an informal reception soon after they come. This may include a gift of cash, equipment needed in the home, or some other practical expression of Christian love.

7

The Ordinances
of the Church

ORDINANCES are established rites or ceremonies. Baptists believe that the Lord has given two to His church—baptism and the Lord's Supper. We do not refer to them as sacraments, as do the Romanists and some others, for that term is used to indicate "a visible sign instituted by Jesus Christ to confer Grace, or Divine Life, on those who worthily receive it." The Word does not promise grace, or life, through these, but commands them to be observed as memorials.

The Roman Church observes seven sacraments: baptism, confirmation, the eucharist, matrimony, penance, holy orders and extreme unction. There is no Biblical support for such practice.

A few small groups practice foot washing as an ordinance. This does not have foundation. It was not so understood by the early church. It was not further developed as a doctrine or practice in the Scripture beyond its mention in John 13. Still more significantly, we believe the Lord denied this in the immediate context. When Peter challenged the Lord in John 13:6, resisting the idea that the Lord should wash the servants' feet, the Lord said (v. 7): "What I do thou knowest not now; but thou shalt know hereafter." Peter certainly understood the outward form and indication of humility. He did not understand the true significance of the washing of water by the Word that the Lord is carrying on (Eph. 5:25, 26). Nor did he understand our responsibility to seek the deliverance of each other from the defilement of daily sins. Galatians 6:1 teaches this truth in another figure: "Brethren, if a man be overtaken in a fault, ye which are spiritual, restore such an one in the spirit of meekness; considering thyself, lest thou also be tempted." This is a holy, humbling occupation which we are commanded to exercise toward each other, but not as an ordinance.

The Lord established baptism and the Lord's Supper as the two rites, or ceremonies, to be observed by His church. He knew the practical value of such repeated enactments of truth. Each time we witness a baptism we are reminded tangibly of our union with Christ as we are identified with Him in His death, burial and resurrection. Each time we participate in the Lord's Supper we are reminded of our communion with Him. These practical reminders should produce renewed devotion to our blessed Lord.

The Lord did not suggest these ceremonies. He commanded them! He said: ". . . This do . . ." (1 Cor. 11:24); "Go . . . teach . . . baptizing . . ." (Matt. 28:19). These ordinances are His orders, and we should observe them as sacred, God-given responsibilities.

Baptism

What does it mean?   As is commonly known, the word *baptize* is simply the Greek word *baptizo* adapted to an English form. Scholars, with few exceptions, whether Baptists or non-Baptists, whether ancient or modern, agree that the word means "to dip or to immerse." It is significant to observe that the Greek church always has immersed and still does (in spite of the false doctrine that has grown up around its practice).

Furthermore, the early church so understood the Lord, for it immersed. There were no known exceptions during the first two centuries. Pouring was allowed in the third century for the bedfast and was called clinic baptism. There is no justification of this practice in the Scripture. It sprang out of expediency, in an effort to make possible the "baptism" of some who probably could not be immersed at the time. A doctrinal error that held baptism to be essential to salvation was creeping into the churches. This gave wholly unjustified weight to the plea for compromise in the practice of baptism.

In spite of serious doctrinal errors that multiplied through the centuries, immersion was understood to be the meaning and mode of baptism by practically all Christendom for fully thirteen centuries. I have seen a large baptistry in the Roman cathedral in Pisa, Italy, which was completed about A.D. 1118.

Most of the leaders and denominations that practice sprinkling or pouring instead of immersion will frankly admit that *baptizo* means immersion, and that the early church practiced immersion. Usually their arguments which seek to justify their present position boil down to: "It is not the form that is important; it is the spirit of the act." But this attitude involves them even more seriously, as we shall now see.

Why is it important?   The spirit, or significance, of the act of baptism is as clear as the meaning of the word, and it seals the importance of the form.

Just as baptism in the Spirit (1 Cor. 12:13) adds believers in our Lord Jesus Christ to the Church which is His Body, so water baptism is the means by which believers are publicly inducted into discipleship (Matt. 28:19, 20) and added to the local church.

These two truths are somewhat interwoven in the opening verses of Romans 6. It is the work of the Holy Spirit, by His baptism, to add us organically to Christ. We are then properly immersed in water, thus being buried in the likeness of His death and raised in the likeness of His resurrection. The ceremony of baptism is unquestionably designed to typify our burial and resurrection with Christ. Only immersion can be such a symbol. All other modes are without significance and become a meaningless "initiation" into Christendom.

The Lord Jesus confirmed this significance in baptism in the unusual statement in Matthew 3:15. John objected to baptizing Jesus, saying: "I have need to be baptized of thee, and comest thou to me?" Jesus answered: "Suffer it to be so now: for thus it becometh us to fulfil all righteousness." This statement was a riddle to me until someone long ago pointed out that "us" in the sentence must apply to the Trinity. It is the same situation as in the words of Genesis 1:26: ". . . Let *us* make man in our image . . . ," and Genesis 11:6, 7: "And the LORD said . . . let *us* go down. . . ." The words in Matthew 3:15 are in perfect harmony with Romans 1:16 and 17, which say that in the gospel of Christ (the good news of His death, burial and resurrection—1 Corinthians 15:1-4) is the righteousness of God revealed! So Christ declared that as He was to be buried and raised in baptism, thus, in His actual death, burial and resurrection, the entire Godhead was engaged in fulfilling all righteousness.

The imagery involved in immersion is very important. It pictures Christ's death, burial and resurrection for us and our identification with Him in this threefold experience. Therefore, though probably without intending to do so, those who "spiritualize" baptism minimize the reality of His death, burial and resurrection.

Some insist upon immersing in *running water*. However, there is no Biblical significance involved in this. While some were thus baptized, it was only because that was an available place. John baptized in Aenon because there was *much* water (not running water). (See John 3:23.)

Furthermore, baptism is important because Christ commanded it! Whether or not we understand it or agree with it, it is "law" to the believer's instructed heart because it is His will! Those who neglect or refuse baptism are disobedient to Him. It is not merely a religious rite.

Who should be baptized?

1. No babies should be baptized. This is contrary to all the Word. The Lord's invitation to suffer the little children to come to Him has no bearing on this. Baptism is not under consideration, and no water is in evidence. The argument based upon household baptism is groundless. It is true that all in the household of the Philippian jailor were baptized, but it is also true that no babies were there! The Word was preached to all who were in the house, and all who were there believed (Acts 16:30-34)! Naturally, therefore, they were all baptized. As a matter of fact, it is interesting to note the fact that *all* were baptized! No one seemed to suggest that this was not important, or that he was not sure just what to do about it!

2. The Word is clear as crystal on this basic fact: Believe and be baptized! See such statements: "Then they that gladly received his word were baptized . . ." (Acts 2:41). "But when they believed . . . they were baptized . . ." (Acts 8:12). "Can any man forbid water, that these should not be baptized, which have received the Holy Ghost as well as we?" (Acts 10:47). ". . . He . . . was baptized, he and all his, straightway . . . believing in God with all his house" (Acts 16:33, 34). See also Acts 19:1-5, where Paul pointed out to some disciples of John the Baptist in Ephesus, that while they had been baptized by John in his baptism unto repentance, they should believe on Christ and be baptized unto Him. They believed and were baptized!

Those who are baptized must be believers in Christ. Baptism is not valid, even by immersion, if the person immersed is not saved. The confession of the act is false at such a time. It is proper and necessary to obedience that he be baptized after being saved. This is not, as some object, "being baptized again"; the first immersion was not baptism.

It is not only important that men be saved before baptism, but it is vital that men be baptized after being saved! Many are delaying because of fear, others because of neglect, still others because of pride. Peter thought this was important. "And he commanded them to be baptized . . ." (Acts 10:48). Too frequently we hear that baptism is not essential to salvation and therefore should not be given prominence in our preaching or practice. It is not essential to our salvation, but it is essential to our obedience! It is crassly selfish to argue that nothing is important but what affects my salvation. *Everything is important that is the will of God and pleases Him!*

3. People should not be baptized who are not coming into the

membership of the local church. Obviously there may be exceptions in some such instance, as the eunuch in Acts 8 or the Philippian jailer in Acts 16. No churches were there! Such a situation may still prevail in remote areas or mission fields before a local church is organized.

Certainly the common practice of converts is to join hearts and hands with fellow believers, as recorded in Acts 2:41, 42 and 47: "Then they that gladly received his word were baptized: and the same day there were added unto them about three thousand souls. And they continued stedfastly. . . . And the Lord added to the church daily such as should be saved."

The New Testament certainly teaches that if there is a Bible-believing church, the new convert should be baptized and come into the fellowship of that church. Under every ordinary circumstance, failure to do so robs the convert of the Biblical responsibilities that are his in attendance, administration, tithing, etc., and frees him from proper restraint of Biblical discipline. This policy in practice actually develops many "church tramps" who are little or no good to the cause of Christ, but who "flit here and there" whenever another pasture looks greener.

My mother used to press home the point, "What kind of a group would this be if each member acted as you do?" Many times that is a revealing and embarrassing question! What kind of church would we have if no one joined but kept footloose? Every Christian has a responsibility to support a New Testament church, and he cannot do so adequately if he is not a member. I have known some of these "nonmembers" to be very embarrassed in doing personal work and seeking to bring people under the sound of the gospel, when they were asked, "Do you belong to that church?" "Why not?" These are good questions and hard to answer!

Who should do the baptizing?   First, we believe the local church is the logical Biblical authority by which the work of the Lord is administered. No other organization has been charged with this task. If baptism is performed through a local church, there is reason to expect things to be done decently and in order. The entrance into public discipleship must properly be authorized by the same authority that holds the right to remove unworthy individuals by discipline. This is exclusively the right of the local New Testament church. If any individual or any group apart from a church undertakes to administer the ordinances, all manner of confusion results. No records are kept; no standards are maintained; no discipline is exercised. We do not believe that missions, schools, Bible conferences or other such groups should undertake this work which belongs properly to the church. Baptists have held this position consistently through the centuries.

Second, the one performing the baptism under the supervision of the local church is usually the pastor, but this need not be so. The church may readily authorize any of its members to do this. Certainly no one need be hindered from obeying the Lord in baptism simply because the pastor is absent.

Communion

Before His departure, the Lord established a service which may properly be called Communion (1 Cor. 10:16) or the Lord's Supper (1 Cor. 11:20). There is a considerable range of emphasis upon some of the details of the administration of this memorial feast, even among Baptists. The fact that the local church is independent and sovereign in the conduct of its own affairs makes it possible to differ in some details and still love one another! Each church must give answer to the Lord for faithfulness in this important matter, but allow sister churches to do the same thing!

What errors are common?   Some common, serious errors are held in some sections of Christendom. The Romanists teach that when the bread or wafer is blessed by them, it becomes the literal body of Christ. This is called *transubstantiation*. They base this upon Christ's words, ". . . This is my body, which is broken for you. . . ." That He was speaking in a figure is evident to us now and was so understood by His disciples then. He stood before them, whole and intact, when He spoke these words. He did not in any sense give, or offer to give, His literal flesh. This error actually involves the awful implication that His body is broken again and again as often as they conduct the mass. In fact, it is taught that the mass is a sacrifice for sins. But the Scripture declares: "But this man [Christ], after he had offered one sacrifice for sins for ever, sat down on the right hand of God. . . . For by one offering he hath perfected for ever them that are sanctified" (Heb. 10:12, 14).

The Lutherans have a similar doctrine, somewhat modified, known as *consubstantiation,* in which they teach that both the literal bread and the literal body exist together in the wafer which they serve.

There is a far too common feeling with many people, even in churches where such error is not taught, that somehow the eating of this Communion will produce a special sanctity within them, or even result in their salvation. Nothing could be farther from the truth as we shall see in the following points.

What does it mean?   As baptism symbolizes the believer's *union* with Christ, so the Lord's Supper symbolizes his *communion* with Christ. Baptism, scripturally administered, is a single act, just as union with Christ is an already accomplished, never-to-be-repeated act. The Lord's Supper is regularly repeated, just as our communion with Him is a constantly enjoyed experience in the normal Christian life.

The Lord's Supper is a memorial feast. We eat the bread and drink the cup, as Christ says, "in remembrance of me" (1 Cor. 11:24, 25). By this feast we "shew the Lord's death till he come" (v. 26). When we, as obedient believers, participate in the Communion service, we manifest a mutual faith and fellowship in His death for us (1 Cor. 10:16, 17).

Why is it important?   First of all, it is important because our Lord says, "Take, eat: . . . this do . . ." (1 Cor. 11:24, 25). Whatever He commands is vital.

Second, this feast has been designed in His infinite wisdom to have several very beneficial effects on the believer.

1. Self-examination should be practiced faithfully before Communion (v. 28). The realization that we are coming to think upon His death for us should be ample cause to search our hearts and lives and to confess any selfishness, greed, bitterness, uncleanness or sin of any sort. While it is not wholesome for a believer to be introspective and think upon himself with regard to either his successes or his sins, it is crucial that we have periods of self-examination and confession. The Lord's Supper calls us back to this needed exercise again and again.

2. Through this ordinance we bear public testimony of our faith in Christ Who died for our sins. No one has any right to participate in this service who does not believe that he is redeemed by the precious blood of Christ. Were it not such tragic blasphemy, it would be amusing to see the inconsistency of the modernists who deny the blood of Christ, yet who gather around a "Communion table." Scripturally observed, this feast is a solemn, silent sermon. I have known souls who were saved when they remained to witness this service. Through this life-sized object lesson they realized the provision that a God of love had made for them in the death of Christ.

3. The Lord's Supper brings vividly to our minds the sufferings of Christ as His body was broken and His blood shed for us. These are basic truths from which our minds and hearts may stray in the pressures of life and the consideration of more complex doctrinal truths. Because of the fickleness of our hearts, there is always the danger that our minds will be corrupted from "the simplicity that is in Christ" (2 Cor. 11:3). If frequently and reverently we come face to face with the

One Who suffered for us, and we think upon His sacrifice there at Calvary, even Satan is confounded in his efforts to divert our affections toward the world. As we eat and drink in remembrance of Him and discern His body in the symbols of the bread and cup, our love for Christ must be stimulated.

4. The Lord said we are to keep this memorial feast "till I come." Therefore, every time we gather at the Table, we are properly reminded of His return for us; our love and anticipation are again encouraged. We look back to Calvary and rejoice in our redemption; and we look forward to His coming and rejoice at the prospect of seeing Him face to face!

Who should participate?   Obviously, no one who does not know Christ can remember Him at the Lord's Table. To be saved through faith in Him is the minimum essential.

The Corinthian believers were backslidden and careless; they were making this a common feast. For this grievous sin of eating and drinking without discerning the Lord's body, some of the people were sick and others had died as a divine judgment. Read 1 Corinthians 11:29-34. This is a very solemn portion. It should sober our hearts concerning this ordinance. It ought not to be taken lightly. Not only should sinners refrain, but so also should believers who are walking in any unconfessed sin.

Baptism logically precedes the Lord's Table, although no one verse in the Word commands this order. The apostles baptized promptly after conversion, so those who came to the Lord's Table were already baptized. Furthermore, as union with Christ precedes communion with Him, so the symbols of these blessed facts belong in that logical order. This is further indicated in Matthew 28:19 and 20 in the order there outlined: make disciples, baptize, teach them to observe all things Christ commanded.

Who should administer the ordinance?   Since the local church is the only Biblically recognized group in charge of the stewardship of spiritual things, Baptists have always contended that this ordinance should be administered by a church and not by schools, conferences or individuals.

The pastor should not carry the communion to individuals and administer it personally. This cannot help but lead to looseness of administration and even to schism.

It is not necessary for the pastor to be present, for the church has a right to ask any spiritually qualified brother in Christ to act.

It is a serious responsibility for a church to be a custodian of such symbols of sacred truth. Each member needs to review his own obedience to these ordinances and to cooperate with the church in carrying out Biblically God's orders on these things.

What elements are to be used?   J. Irving Reese gave helpful teaching on the Lord's Supper. We quote his remarks concerning the elements:

> The elements, which are unfermented wine and unleavened bread, preach mighty sermons. The wine speaks of the uncorrupted blood of the Lord Jesus (Psa. 16:10); the unleavened bread, His sinless body. Leaven in the Scriptures is a type of sin (Exod. 12:14, 15; 1 Pet. 2:22; 1 Cor. 5:6-8; Matt. 16:6-12). It is most improper, if not blasphemous, to use ordinary raised bread for the Supper. Matzoth, the Jewish Passover bread, is very available today and comparatively inexpensive. Even a small church can secure it. It can be purchased at a Jewish grocery store, especially at Passover time, or a church supply house.[1] If Matzoth cannot be obtained, plain, unsalted soda crackers will serve the purpose, rather than leavened bread.

1. Also available in grocery stores.

8

The Discipline of the Church

ONE OF THE MOST neglected doctrines of the Word of God is church discipline. It is encouraging to learn from our missionaries that our national churches in other lands are more faithful to these scriptural teachings than are most of our churches in the homeland.

The neglect of church discipline is in line with the general trend in our current social and educational development. The lack of adequate authority and discipline in homes, schools, governments and churches can certainly be blamed as a major factor in the lawlessness and delinquency on every hand. Bible-believing churches ought not to be a part of this worldly philosophy.

The success of the apostates in capturing the organizations and churches of the great denominations is due largely to the failure of the past generation in our churches to judge and remove unbelievers instead of allowing them to multiply and gain control. We need to learn from their costly lesson the urgency of dealing with sin. To fail to do so not only allows it to become entrenched, but grieves the Holy Spirit and thus robs us of His power and enabling to discern and resist sin. May the Lord revive within us a willingness to obey His Word in this responsibility of discipline.

The attitude which accompanies the work of discipline is vital. Probably an undue harshness of attitude was previously one of the causes for the modern disuse of this practice. The Lord help us to hold the truth in love! (See Hebrews 12:6 and 7.)

Biblical Reasons for Discipline

As we present some of the Scriptures on this point, we warn that proper attitudes, objectives and methods must mark the people as well as the official actions of the church. Patience and impartiality must be evident in all our dealings with those caught in sin.

Without laying claim to an exhaustive treatment on this subject, we point out five basic reasons for discipline.

Immorality.   In 1 Corinthians 5 immorality is declared to demand reproof and refusal of fellowship as long as the sin is continued and unconfessed. Moral looseness is so prevalent that even the most sheltered individuals are aware of it. To those who deal realistically with the men of the world, the situation is appalling. It has invaded even the most fundamental churches and moves quite openly without even a mild reproof in many cases. The church cannot retain its power and testimony unless it deals with moral uncleanness.

False doctrine.   False doctrine cannot be tolerated. Obviously this does not refer to differences of interpretation of various verses nor to minor matters based on personal opinions. But when the honor and truth of God's Word is at stake, we dare not compromise. Read 1 Timothy 6:1-5 and note: ". . . If any man teach otherwise, and consent not to wholesome words, even the words of our Lord Jesus Christ, and to the doctrine which is according to godliness; . . . from such withdraw thyself." In 1 Timothy 1:19 and 20 Paul named two men, Hymenaeus and Alexander, who had departed from the faith. He dealt with them as he commanded the Corinthians to do with the man taken in fornication. (See also 2 Timothy 2:16-18.)

Disorderly walk.   A disorderly walk requires discipline (2 Thess. 3:6, 14). This involves a walk that is in disobedience to the Word. Paul says, ". . . Withdraw yourselves from every brother that walketh disorderly, and not after the tradition [that is, the teaching] which he received of us. . . . And if any man obey not our word by this epistle, note that man, and have no company with him. . . ." This is further colored by the command (2:15): ". . . Stand fast, and hold the traditions [teachings] which ye have been taught, whether by word, or our epistle." Paul was not commanding to withdraw fellowship merely from those who would not work (3:11-13), as some claim. He was commanding such action toward all brethren in Christ who persisted in disobedience to any apostolic and Biblical teaching. He spoke of oral commandments or teaching (2:15) because at that time much of the New Testament was unwritten, and God had given to the apostles special gifts of knowledge and authority by which the early churches were guided until the Scriptures were completed. Now the Word of God is the sole standard of faith and practice, and no oral pronouncements of pastors, councils or popes can bind the conscience. It is common and commendable, however, to define our doctrinal convictions in brief statements of faith. These have no authority, but they clarify by explanation and must be subject to proof from the Word.

Divisions.   Divisions contrary to Biblical doctrine demand discipline. Read Paul's words in Romans 16:17 and 18 and again in Titus 3:10. Many a church would have been saved endless heartache and loss of power by exercising Biblical discipline upon troublemakers who cause divisions that are contrary to Biblical doctrine. As these verses declare, they are people who serve their own selfish ends and who are often eventually discovered to be harboring serious sin.

On this point, grave caution must be taken not to use these verses simply to remove those who differ from us. The charge is against those who are at odds with the Word.

This charge of troublemakers is often leveled by the liberals or the compromisers at those who teach Biblical separation from both sin and apostasy. As a matter of fact, these liberals are the ones who are disobeying the Scripture and who are causing the divisions contrary to the doctrine.

Unrepentant attitude.   An unrepentant attitude over sin must be judged. Matthew 18:15-17 teaches that a man who will not hear the church in its effort to accomplish a reconciliation between brethren is to be treated as "an heathen man and a publican." That is, he is to be refused fellowship until he repents of his sin and gives evidence of his subjection to the Word of God.

Biblical Attitudes in Discipline

If sin is reproved with harshness and bitterness, the reproof itself involves sin. If the attitude is simply to "throw him out of the church," it is far from Biblical. It is not natural to the flesh to do anything but strive under such conditions; and there is grave danger that in the heat of trials we may fall into fleshly attitudes. The Lord is never honored by this, and such actions must be avoided.

Obviously, church discipline should not be implemented over trivial differences. Furthermore, we may often willingly suffer wrong for Christ's sake if the offense is personal. We certainly are to do this rather than take a brother to court before *the world* (1 Cor. 6:1-8). However, there are many motives besides self-vindication for bringing offenders to account for their wrongs. Failure to do so is often unfair to them, the Lord and the church.

Spirituality, humility, meekness.   Spirituality, humility and meekness must mark those who undertake to deal scripturally with a fallen brother. Galatians 6:1 is very clear. Spirituality is not some mysterious, ethereal quality of which one boasts! It is simply yieldedness to, and the fullness of, the Holy Spirit.

Uncompromising stand against sin.   A firm, uncompromising stand against sin is essential. There is no necessary conflict between this attitude and that expressed in point one. Jesus Christ rebuked and resisted sin with tremendous force as He drove the money changers from the temple (John 2:13-17). None but the most blasphemous unbeliever would charge Him with a lack of spirituality! He was holy. See Paul's command concerning the carnal teachers in Crete: ". . . Wherefore rebuke them sharply, that they may be sound in the faith" (Titus 1:13). "Them that sin rebuke before all, that others also may fear" (1 Tim. 5:20).

Love.   Love for brethren who are still in sin is a must! "Yet count him not as an enemy, but admonish him as a brother" (2 Thess. 3:15), is the Biblical attitude. The Lord manifested this tenderness toward a wayward Peter. Love is a great solvent. By it the Spirit of God will dissolve the bitterness in some hearts, whereas argument and evidence will only harden them.

Many such instances have come to my attention. A pastor had dealt for hours with a man who had fallen into serious sin, but he had made no apparent progress in leading the man to confess and forsake his sin. The burden pressed so upon the pastor's heart under the Spirit's ministry that, unexpectedly and unbidden, tears flowed freely. In a few moments the other heart was broken, and tears and confession came with the observation: "I never realized that I had a pastor who cared that much for my soul."

Obviously such attitudes cannot be forced; they must be real if God is to bless! Furthermore, not all tears manifest real Christian love, nor is love always manifest in tears. But we should love our brethren enough to weep over them when they are out in the world and in sin. Read 1 Corinthians 13 often.

Forgiveness.   Forgiveness to those who repent and confess is a basic law of the Word. Read the Lord's words as recorded in Luke 17:3 and 4. Little wonder, in the light of our own haughty, unforgiving hearts, the next words of His disciples were, "Increase our faith."

The absolute standard of forgiveness is set before us in Ephesians 4:32: "And be ye kind one to another, tenderhearted, forgiving one another, even as God for Christ's sake hath forgiven you." His forgiveness to us was not of the sort, "I shall forgive, but I can never forget." He forgave us fully, freely and finally.

It is true, however, that we were not assured of His forgiveness until our sins were acknowledged and we recognized that He had judged the sin, paid its full penalty at Calvary, and proclaimed to us that forgiveness through His infinite grace.

It is also true that a brother who has sinned should not expect his brethren to merely whitewash his sins; he must be willing to acknowledge them and accept forgiveness as brotherly grace.

The blending of these four attitudes into one attitude is essential. Spirituality in our relationship to God, uncompromising opposition in our attitude toward sin, love and compassion for those ensnared in sin and gracious forgiveness to those who confess their sin are all the results of the work of the Spirit. They should exist simultaneously and perpetually in each of our lives. As they do, church quarrels will cease; personal differences with attending heartaches will disappear. The world around will know we are born of God because we love our brethren.

This is not idealistic. The Spirit of God can and will produce such attitudes in us if we yield to Him. These things are the fruit of the Spirit; they are not attained by willpower. On the contrary, the absence of these attitudes is sin, stemming out of self-will. We need to be candid with ourselves and judge ourselves before we undertake to help our brethren!

Biblical Objectives in Discipline

Biblical attitudes should, of course, be wisely administered with Biblical objectives. If these are properly understood, there should not be the prejudice against church discipline that currently is widespread. We suggest four that are basic:

Obedience to the Word of God. Whether or not we understand or agree, we are under obligation to our Lord to obey His Word. The official judgment and punishment of sin is clearly commanded in the Book. Many times we ignore or excuse the sin long after patience and grace have been fully exercised.

Removal of the defilement of sin. As leaven leavens the whole lump (1 Cor. 5:6), so sin permeates and defiles the entire group. Achan's sin, as recorded in Joshua 7, reveals God's attitude. While the sin was unjudged, Israel was defeated. Victory did not come until Achan was put to death for his sin. God commands in 1 Corinthians 5:7, "Purge out therefore the old leaven. . . ." God is dishonored if we allow sin to remain unjudged in our individual lives or in the church. He dwells within us, and He is holy! He is grieved and offended with sin. Putting away evil, therefore, is basic to His pleasure in us and to His honor in our testimony.

Restraint of others.   In 1 Timothy 5:20 this principle is laid down, "Them that sin rebuke before all, that others also may fear."

Modern psychology objects to a negative approach and opposes commandments and warnings. God's Word does not support such a theory, for the theory ignores the awful fact of a depraved human nature. It would be ideal if men could be encouraged to live godly lives without any warning of judgment upon ungodliness. But to suppose they will do so is idealistic and contrary to all observation, as well as to Scripture. God warns of impending judgment and says, "It is a fearful thing to fall into the hands of the living God" (Heb. 10:31). "Because there is wrath, beware . . ." (Job 36:18).

If sin goes unjudged in a church, we are thereby inviting others to become self-indulgent. It will not do to plead "love" as a basis for neglect. We have all seen parents whose philosophy was, "I love my children too much to punish them." And we have seen a distressing number of such children grow up to be punished by state, church, conscience or God for a life of undisciplined self-will. God does not put love and punishment in opposition to each other. He says, "For whom the Lord loveth he chasteneth. . . ." Read Hebrews 12:5-11.

The church has a solemn responsibility to restrain sin by proper discipline. If we do not exercise the judgment, the Lord will. "For if we would judge ourselves, we should not be judged. But when we are judged, we are chastened of the Lord, that we should not be condemned with the world" (1 Cor. 11:31, 32).

Restore the erring brother.   "Brethren, if a man be overtaken in a fault, ye which are spiritual, restore such an one . . ." (Gal. 6:1).

Too frequently when discipline has been exercised by a church, the attitude has been, "Well, that's that," as though the final chapter had been written by the removal of the disobedient. This was not Paul's viewpoint as he wrote in 2 Corinthians 2:6-8: "Sufficient to such a man is this punishment, which was inflicted of many. So that contrariwise ye ought rather to forgive him, and comfort him, lest perhaps such a one should be swallowed up with overmuch sorrow. Wherefore I beseech you that ye would confirm your love toward him."

We do not punish our children to get even with them, but to correct them. So ought the church to judge sin with the humble, earnest prayer that God will grant repentance and restore the soul to His fellowship and to ours.

Biblical Methods in Discipline

Sometimes pastors have assumed the power to remove offenders from the church. Sometimes the deacons have done so. Neither practice is Biblical.

Many times churches have voted members out of the church without dealing with them personally, or without giving them an opportunity to defend themselves before the church. Since members are received into the membership by vote of the church, they cannot be dismissed without such a vote. Since the members have covenanted together in this holy relationship, the mutual covenant cannot be severed without mutual consent, unless it is evident and certain that one of the parties to the covenant has violated it. Every precaution should be taken to avoid false accusations and unfair judgments.

Some vital principles are laid down in Matthew 18:15-17. This portion is rejected by some as not appropriate for the church, which was not fully instituted until Pentecost. However, two chapters earlier (16:18), the Lord said He would build His church. These to whom He spoke were the men who in a brief time became the charter members of the first churches. He Himself said: "Tell it unto the church." If the instruction book for your car comes from the press before your car comes from the assembly line, it is no less authoritative if the one who wrote the book produced the car!

The following well-known, but often neglected, principles are given clearly and concisely in Matthew 18; they are supported with an abundance of other New Testament Scripture.

Seek reconciliation. The responsibility to seek reconciliation rests with the offended, not the offender. "Moreover if thy brother shall trespass against thee, go and tell him his fault between thee and him alone: if he shall hear thee, thou hast gained thy brother." If this is practiced, it will quickly check gossip, misunderstanding, bitterness and subsequent schism.

The same standard is stated in Galatians 6:1. It is the one walking with the Lord who initiates the effort to rescue the brother at fault. The latter may not have the desire, and certainly does not have the discernment, to open the matter while out of fellowship. James 5:19 and 20 indicate the same procedure.

Witnesses. Witnesses were to be taken if the private effort failed.

This demonstrates sincerity of purpose and gives a second opportunity to the guilty to confess his wrong. It also provides witnesses if the matter must come to the church for settlement. These efforts should be genuine and bathed in prayer for the Lord's power and blessing to be at work.

Go to the church.   If the sin still continues, the problem must come to the church. This was the situation in 1 Corinthians 5. The church's responsibility is further emphasized in 1 Corinthians 6:1-8. If the man is guilty and will not confess and forsake the sin, he must be refused fellowship if the sin is serious. This includes all the rights of his church membership, such as leadership, voting and Communion.

Restoration.   Restoration, according to 2 Corinthians 2:6-8, should follow public confession and forsaking of the sin. If the sin was serious, the party, though fully forgiven, should not expect to be restored to a place of leadership until he has proved himself. On the other hand, he should be genuinely welcomed and not be treated with suspicion.

Warnings About Church Discipline

Haste and harshness should never exist. In 2 Timothy 2:24-26 and 4:2, a right spirit was evidenced in dealing with the wayward.

Partiality must be avoided, and this is difficult. God does not regard one above another. Personal relationship to friends or relatives poses a real strain on our faithfulness to God in this matter.

If a member is under discipline by one church, no church of like faith and order should receive into membership the person under discipline until the matter is settled within the disciplining church. To receive such a member (one under discipline) before the matter is settled is to frustrate the whole force and purpose of discipline.

There should be faithful teaching in the church upon this theme in times when discipline is not a problem, so when it is, men will be fortified with the truth they gained when there was no prejudice or strife. These principles of obedience must be kept free from personalities.

9

The Ministry
of the Church

SOON AFTER ENTERING the ministry, I heard a man who had graduated from a modernistic seminary say, "The primary business of the church is to equalize the wealth of the world in the hands of the people." He may have had good motives, but he had poor theology! He did not find this objective for the church's ministry in the Book. Even the Lord Jesus said, "For the poor always ye have with you . . ." (John 12:8). Certainly Christians should do all that is possible to comfort and relieve poverty and suffering, but the primary ministry of the church is not social and economic. Wonderful social and economic reactions result from a Biblical ministry, but they are the by-products of lives transformed by divine grace as the church preaches the message of personal salvation through faith in Jesus Christ.

Probably nothing about the church is more confused in the minds of men than its objective. What is the purpose of the church? Why did the Lord build the church?

The liberal, with his social gospel, has certainly missed the purpose of God. Our Lord did not send the church forth to raise social standards and make unregenerate men happy in the midst of their sin. *He changes men.* Then conditions change because the men are different. Man's problem is sin. It has cut him off from God and His blessings. No amount of education, culture, economic security or religion will restore man's peace and happiness. He must be reconciled to God. Sin must be dealt with on the basis of the blood of Christ shed for the remission of sins!

The social gospel is commonly heard in a majority of liberal churches. It is socialism in religion. It is falsely called "the Kingdom of

God'' by such theological liberals as the late E. Stanley Jones and G. Bromley Oxnam.

Leaders of the National Council of Churches of Christ now call this social action and foster lawlessness in the form of illegal actions in marches, sit-ins, etc. Colin W. Williams, NCCC leader in the field of evangelism, told a news conference in Miami Beach, in December, 1966 (*Crusader,* March 1967), "It is no longer possible to distinguish between a personal conversion experience and a change of social attitudes." (In context, this referred to such social action as mentioned above.)

We need to be awake to these errors, for they are totally opposed to the Biblical ministry of the church. It is urgent that we be familiar with the divine objectives in this age if we are to be intelligent workers together with God.

God forbid that we should be lacking in compassion toward the needy. With acts of love we can melt many hearts that have remained as flint under the preaching of truth. But may we never forget that without the truth, even a melted heart can never be saved!

While many aspects of responsibility are laid upon the church, we believe its ministry centers in three fundamental duties: evangelization, edification and glorification.

Evangelize the Sinners

This is basic in the very nature of Christianity. It is a missionary faith. No denomination or individual church has ever flourished long without an evangelistic fervor. It is necessary to keep this aspect of our ministry in balance with other responsibilities, but it must never become secondary!

A burden for the salvation of others is one of the first and finest evidences of salvation in one who has just confessed Christ. This concern to share with his fellowmen the good news that has just transformed his life is a logical reaction; but it is more than that. It is a supernatural reaction in the regenerated heart, produced by the Holy Spirit. The burden goes beyond carnal enthusiasm to sacrificial devotion. Soul-winners will bear united testimony that this is true. There is reason to question the spiritual comprehension of a new convert who fails to react in this manner. This work of the Spirit in the hearts of His people is excellent evidence, even though secondary evidence, as to the purpose of the Lord for our ministry.

The commands and instruction of the Word form primary evidence of His will. "Go ye therefore, and teach [literally, make disciples of] all nations . . ." (Matt. 28:19). "And that repentance and remission of sins should be preached in his name among all nations, beginning at Jerusalem. And ye are witnesses of these things" (Luke 24:47, 48). ". . . Ye shall be witnesses unto me . . . unto the uttermost part of the earth" (Acts 1:8). (See other portions, such as Romans 10:12-15.) Acts 13:2, 3, 38 and 39 record the Holy Spirit's action in sending out Barnabas and Paul and the vital evangelistic message they preached. There can be no doubt as to the command of the Word. Neither can there be doubt that the apostles and the early church understood this command and followed it. We submit a few examples of the evidence from the Bible:

Christ Himself set the pattern for evangelism both to individuals and to the multitudes. The four Gospels bear abundant testimony to this fact.

The examples of the apostles and the early church demonstrated evangelism to be a primary ministry of the church.

Peter denounced sin and offered salvation in the major messages recorded in Acts 2, 3, 4 and 10.

"Then *Philip* went down to the city of Samaria, and preached Christ unto them. And the people with one accord gave heed . . ." (Acts 8:5, 6). In verse 26 of the same chapter, he was sent to the desert to lead the Ethiopian eunuch to Christ.

Paul, brought to Christ on the road to Damascus, became one of the world's greatest evangelists. While it is true that he had a great burden for the edification of the church, it is also true that he burned with missionary zeal throughout all his ministry. He declared boldly: "For so hath the Lord commanded us, saying, I have set thee to be a light of the Gentiles, that thou shouldest be for salvation unto the ends of the earth" (Acts 13:47). Throughout the rest of the Book of Acts, we see that Paul's zeal never diminished. Whether beaten, stoned or imprisoned, he seized every opportunity to witness in the next city and the next country "that Jesus was Christ" (Acts 18:5).

Paul had a tremendous burden for the salvation of Israel. He was willing to be accursed for them (Rom. 9:2, 3). His "heart's desire and prayer to God for Israel" was "that they might be saved" (Rom. 10:1). He declared that he was a minister of the gospel, as well as of the mystery (Col. 1:23-29). Paul was a pioneer missionary; he sought to reach where Christ had not been preached rather than to build upon another man's foundation (Rom. 15:19, 20). In the beginning of the Epistle to the Romans he cried: "So, as much as in me is, I am ready to preach the gospel. . . . I am not ashamed of the gospel . . ." (1:15, 16).

Much more is recorded in the Bible, but surely this is sufficient to arouse us from lethargy and to reveal the fallacy of those who imply they have no room in their important ministry for the gospel message! The great apostle to the Gentiles, with all his revelations and teaching ministry, rejoiced in the closing hours of his life that he was appointed a gospel preacher (2 Tim. 1:10, 11).

It is a primary responsibility and a holy privilege to evangelize the lost. Each believer needs to evaluate the measure of his own involvement in this work. Are we seeking opportunities to reach men with the gospel? Are we working in the visitation programs of our churches? Are we witnessing to relatives, neighbors and associates in business, school or social life? Are we supporting enthusiastically the missionary program of our churches? Failure in this vital activity may indicate that we have lost our first love for Christ or are out of fellowship with Him because of sin.

Edify the Saints

The lack of concern about a teaching ministry for building up the saints is tragic and widespread. One frequently hears sincere, but mistaken, people say: "Get people saved. That is the important thing. The Lord will take care of them." But these enthusiastic remarks will not diminish the responsibility laid on us in God's Word. It is crucial that men be won! But there is no reason to suppose we can improve upon God's method and win more souls by majoring on part of God's will and neglecting the rest. The Lord is as able to save men without the ministry of His servants as He is to edify the saved without such ministry. *The fact is, He has chosen men to be His instruments both in winning the lost and in edifying the saints! We are responsible.*

The same Lord Who said make disciples said in the same breath that we are to baptize them and to teach them to observe all things that He has commanded. This was the method used by the early churches as witnessed in the Book of Acts. The truth prospered; the churches multiplied; vast numbers were saved during that first century as the apostolic message was proclaimed with apostolic methods.

The apostle Paul was not satisfied to conduct an evangelistic campaign and then leave it up to the Lord to care for the babes in Christ! Churches were established (Acts 14:23), and subsequent care was given to confirm and establish these local churches. Paul traveled extensively to see personally that this was done (Acts 15:41; 16:4, 5). This, of course, necessitated that the converts first be baptized, and this he also did. (See Acts 16:14, 15, 30-34.) Peter, too, observed this principle. At the house of Cornelius he commanded them to be baptized after they confessed faith in Christ (Acts 10:47, 48). Philip was also faithful in this, both at Samaria and with the eunuch (Acts 8:12, 38, 39).

It is not enough to lead men to Christ! That is primary; but there is more! Christ said, ". . . Feed my lambs. . . . Feed my sheep. . . . Feed my sheep" (John 21:15-17). God has committed to us the care of His flock! "Take heed . . . to all the flock, over the which the Holy Ghost hath made you overseers, to feed the church of God . . ." (Acts 20:28). It is true that the Lord is the Shepherd and Bishop of our souls (1 Pet. 2:25), but He has committed the care of His flock to us in certain respects, and He will hold us responsible for His sheep.

Our responsibility to edify one another may be considered in four ways.

Instruction.   The saints need instruction, and for this purpose the Lord has not only sent the Holy Spirit and His Word, but has given as gifts to the churches evangelists, pastors and teachers (Eph. 4:11-15). (It appears that the apostles and prophets ceased with the apostolic era. They are no longer needed since the Word of God has been given.)

The saints need the ministry of teaching and should attend faithfully the preaching of the Word (Heb. 10:24, 25). We should cry out to the Lord to raise up such ministers of the Word out of our churches, and every care should be taken to sustain them as well as to train them in His ministry.

This teaching should encompass the whole counsel of God, including that which is *needed* as well as that which is *pleasing!* Paul practiced this (Acts 20:27-31). Often the teaching that is most needed is that which is least desired, but the wise and faithful servant of God will not shun his duty. The church long ago was faced with certain dangers that do not now threaten us. False teachers denied the humanity of Christ! It was necessary to repudiate that error and to strengthen the saints in the truth. John was doing that in his first epistle, and Paul in his epistle to the Colossians. Now the enemy is affirming the Lord's humanity and denying His deity, and the emphasis of ministry shifts although the same Scriptures constitute the Sword in each battle. Once the attack on the church came from wicked men outside the church. Today they have invaded and betrayed the churches from within, as predicted in 2 Peter 2 and other portions. If we are to be faithful stewards of the truth entrusted to us, we must warn the saints of this danger. This is one of the current issues in our day, and no faithful minister can ignore the teaching of the Word on the Biblical doctrine of separation. Whether popular or unpopular, the saints need the instruction of the whole counsel of God. Paul's letters are packed with teaching vital to us as well as to the saints of his day.

We do not wish to leave the impression that all such instruction must be received from pastors and teachers. Each soul is free to learn directly from the Word of God and through his own daily experiences with the Lord. But we do wish to say that no ministry of evangelists, pastors and teachers is complete and Biblical if it omits areas of revealed truth vital to the spiritual life of the saints.

Encouragement.   The saints need encouragement. A Biblical example is set by the apostle Paul because in most of his letters he opens with commendations and praise when it can be sincerely given. To the Romans, it was rejoicing in their faith (1:8); to the Corinthians, it was praise to the Lord for the grace, gifts and knowledge bestowed on them (1 Cor. 1:4-7); to the Galatians in serious doctrinal error, he gave no commendation; but to the Ephesians he wrote encouragingly of their "faith in the Lord Jesus, and love unto all the saints" (1:15).

The Lord Jesus found opportunity to commend something in each of the seven churches except Laodicea (Rev. 2, 3).

Flattery is unworthy; but many a weary, discouraged heart has taken new hope and strength from honest commendation. ". . . A word spoken in due season, how good is it!" (Prov. 15:23). Such attitudes on the part of brethren to each other, from the pastor to his people or from the people to their pastor can transform the spirit of an entire congregation. There are times when reproof must be given, but let us be gracious and encourage one another more frequently!

Prayer.   The assurance of prayer is another edifying and encouraging thing. The apostle freely practiced this ministry and set before us a good example. Read his prayer for the saints at Philippi (Phil. 1:8-11) and for those at Colosse (Col. 1:9-11). Many other prayers are included in these and others of his epistles.

It is comforting to know that men and women of God are praying for us. The major impact of prayer, however, is not a mere psychological comfort, but the power of God that is brought to bear upon us as we claim His promises and continue faithfully in prayer. Brethren, let us pray for one another.

Cleansing.   The saints need cleansing. Too frequently we fall into disobedience in some matter that affects our own testimony and that of the entire church. It may be a harsh critical spirit, companionship that is unworthy, dress that is improper or a levity and boisterousness that is of the world.

Too frequently when some saint falls into such sin, others begin to gossip instead of pray; they talk to everyone except the erring brother to whom they should go. Thus the saint who needs help is neglected, and the others suffer for their disobedience.

Galatians 6:1 commands: "Brethren, if a man be overtaken in a fault, ye which are spiritual, restore such an one in the spirit of meekness; considering thyself, lest thou also be tempted." We need to exercise that grace toward each other and to give and accept such exhortations to godliness. ". . . Reprove, rebuke, exhort with all longsuffering and doctrine" (2 Tim. 4:2). The Scripture itself is given "for doctrine, for reproof, for correction, for instruction in righteousness: That the man of God may be perfect, throughly furnished unto all good works" (2 Tim. 3:16, 17). If we use it faithfully and skillfully, the saints will be built up in the faith!

These points are summarized in 1 Corinthians 14:3: "But he that prophesieth speaketh unto men to edification, and exhortation, and comfort." It is the will of God that His children should not only be born, but should also grow up. We are to desire the milk of the Word that we may grow (1 Pet. 2:2). We are not to remain as children; we are to grow up (Eph. 4:11-16).

May the Lord increase our desire to hear the cry of spiritual babes in our churches as well as upon the mission fields. But may He spare us from satisfaction with anything less than the obedience and growth of those babes in Christ! We are as responsible to nurture them in Christ as we were responsible to witness to them about Christ.

Glorify the Savior

The glorifying of God is the highest pinnacle of human privilege and responsibility. As men, we are not likely to consider it so. Things which affect our destiny or our comfort and happiness too often take precedence in our thinking. But the Bible is emphatic on this subject.

Conduct.   Our conduct is to be governed by a desire to glorify God. "What? know ye not that your body is the temple of the Holy Ghost which is in you, which ye have of God, and ye are not your own? For ye are bought with a price: therefore glorify God in your body, and in your spirit, which are God's" (1 Cor. 6:19, 20). Our actions are not to be governed by what we think is to our best advantage, but by a responsibility to act for God's glory. "Whether therefore ye eat, or drink, or whatsoever ye do, do all to the glory of God" (1 Cor. 10:31). Many problems in the business and social life of Christians would be quickly settled by this principle. Many professing Christians argue about smoking, theaters, worldly companions and other similar things. They give this feeble defense: "I can't see anything wrong about it." That is negative and wholly inadequate. Is there anything right about it? Will the thing under consideration glorify God? That must be the basis of decision for the spiritual man.

The same principle applies to the decisions of the church. In the calling of a pastor, the election of officers, the disciplining of members, the spending of money, the appraising of a man's ministry, the fellow-shipping with other groups, the determining of a missionary responsibility—in all these things the principle must be: "Not my will, but Thine be done!" We should gladly determine: "He must increase, but I must decrease" (John 3:30).

Rarely have any of us seen churches quarreling unless one or both parties to the quarrel has forsaken the desire to glorify God. Self-will is the stuff from which strife is made.

Confession.   Our confession of Christ and His worthiness should bring glory to Him constantly. This is God's will for all ages, including the present (Eph. 3:21).

We are to acknowledge His authority over us in our preaching, prayer, singing and in all of our attitudes. We are to preach not our-selves, but Christ Jesus the Lord (2 Cor. 4:5).

Our testimony should give glory to the Savior as we confess Him before men. All before whom we live should be made conscious of His great power. They should be made to realize that as Christians we are what we are by the grace of God. The very purpose of the church's existence is "that we should be to the praise of his glory . . ." (Eph. 1:12).

Herod accepted the worship of the people who cried: "It is the voice of a god, and not of a man. And immediately the angel of the Lord smote him, because he gave not God the glory . . ." (Acts 12:22, 23). Contrast the Christ-honoring testimony of Paul and Barnabas in Acts 14:8-15.

Worship.   Worship is the climax of all Christian activity. It is the most neglected part of ministry. Preaching is vital. It brings blessing and salvation to men. Meditation and study are essential for our own growth. Prayer, with intercession and petition, is basic for victory and provision of daily needs. But worship glorifies God. It does not center in what He does for us or what we need. Man is forgotten and the Lord is exalted. Worship focuses on Who God is and upon His holiness, glory, power, wisdom, love and mercy.

Examine some Biblical examples of worship. Read Psalm 95:1-7a; Jude 24 and 25; and Revelation 4:10 and 11. For a few commands and instructions, see Matthew 4:10; John 4:23 and 24; and Philippians 3:3.

Worship is not formalism, nor is it produced by thick carpets, soft music and stained-glass windows. (However, it is not hindered by these things.) Worship springs from redeemed hearts that are overwhelmed with the greatness of our God. We should worship more frequently, alone and in public services.

The primary motive of God in the salvation of men is the glory of Christ, not of men! He is now the Head of a new creation (Rev. 3:14). He is the Firstborn among many brethren (Rom. 8:29). This is the place of honor. He is the One Who inherits the authority and the power.

Let us constantly acknowledge: "Worthy is the Lamb that was slain to receive power, and riches, and wisdom, and strength, and honour, and glory, and blessing." Read Revelation 5:9-14.

10

Music in the Church

THE CHRISTIAN FAITH is a singing faith in a very unique sense. Christ puts into our hearts a joy that overflows beyond words and actions into melody. Well may we sing, "I sing because I'm happy, I sing because I'm free." Music should be a vital part of every Christian gathering. It should constitute a real portion of our testimony, our praise and our worship. It should exercise a major impact on the spiritual life and ministry of the church.

The "music" that is borrowed from the world should be banished from the church. Many songs and choruses in common use today have within them the beat of the jungle and the dance floor. They stimulate the flesh, not the spiritual life. Words of many songs and choruses are light, frivolous, meaningless—utterly unscriptural and unworthy of a place in a Christian service. Pastors and music committees will do well to guard carefully against pollution of the services with such impure music.

A Spiritual Ministry

Music in the church service is a spiritual ministry. Those who play and sing should be spiritual people, even as those who preach. Church music should glorify God. This cannot be done by the unsaved, nor by carnal Christians who are walking in the world, no matter how much musical talent they have. We should never choose our preachers that way, and we ought not thus to select our musicians.

The leadership, organization and personnel in the music department are vital elements. Choir leaders, organists and pianists who pray about and plan their music, with a desire to glorify the Lord, are a real asset to the pastor and to the total ministry of the church. Even if such people have limited ability, they are to be preferred over the most talented whose chief concern is the impression they make on the audience.

It is sometimes said that the choir is the war department of the church. This need never be so. Trouble in the choir is caused by some needless errors and is not necessarily a part of a musical ministry. When such strife develops, it is the result of the carnality of some, or all, of those involved. The strife will come eventually if carnal leadership is tolerated, whether it is in the choir or the cradle roll.

I have no delusions that the following suggestions are comprehensive or infallible. However, they are principles that are spiritually sound. They will help a church develop a choir with a blessed spiritual ministry.

1. Members of the choir should be spiritual members of the church. This is not a place for the unsaved or the stranger.

2. The choir should properly be an organized group with a definite membership. Members may be selected by a capable choir director or a music committee. Choice should be based upon both spiritual and musical qualifications, with consideration being given to a proper balance of the parts of the choir.

Responsibility will be developed in the members if officers are chosen and the organization is conducted in a businesslike manner. High standards should be maintained in attendance, attention and conduct. It should be an honor to serve the Lord in this musical ministry, but one that may be forfeited by disinterest and carelessness.

3. The choir director is a vital key to the spiritual progress of the group. Normally it is most desirable that the leader, man or woman, be a member of the church, not an employed musician from the outside. Essential qualities of a good director are a knowledge of music, genuine spirituality, patience, firm discipline, real humility, happy cooperation with the pastor and music committee, and a clear recognition that the central aspect of the church service is the preaching of God's Word.

Sometimes it is proper for the pastor or someone in his family to direct the choir. However, this should never be done unless it is the result of a lack of other leadership, or is the enthusiastic desire of the choir and church. It is good to spread responsibility as widely as possible without sacrificing spiritual and capable leadership.

4. It is desirable that the ministry of the choir supplement the pastor's ministry as much as possible. The director may well consult the pastor for advice and also observe topics announced in advance.

Good music with a Biblical message is essential. Diction must be good enough so that the congregation understands the words clearly. A good hymn, well sung, may be very helpful, even though well-known to the congregation. However, the church should authorize the purchase of an adequate supply of good choir music to provide the director with a variety of selections. It is wise to avoid music too involved for the ability of the choir, or of such a nature as to appear to be a mere display of talent rather than a spiritual ministry.

5. The pastor should seek to challenge the choir, both personally and publicly, as to the vital importance of its ministry. A good choir deserves encouragement, and a poor one needs it!

6. The choir will profit from time spent in prayer before practice. It may be helpful for the pastor to join in these prayer times now and then.

7. Special musical events, such as Easter and Christmas cantatas, will give helpful incentive to a choir to work faithfully. These special ministries should be times of great spiritual blessing if the music is Christ honoring and is presented capably.

Obviously some of these principles can be attained only a step at a time, but progress in the right direction is encouraging. Some of the suggestions cannot be followed easily where talent is limited. But let us give our very best to the Lord without any taint of jealousy or carnal ambition. Such attitudes are sinful and should be judged if they seek to control us.

". . . Be filled with the Spirit; Speaking to yourselves in psalms and hymns and spiritual songs, singing and making melody in your heart to the Lord" (Eph. 5:18, 19).

11

The Church and Evangelism

EVANGELISM is a primary responsibility of each church. The pastor must teach, challenge and lead the church in aggressive evangelism, even while he edifies the saints and equips them to serve the Lord. As Paul charged Timothy, ". . . Do the work of an evangelist" (2 Tim. 4:5). According to tradition, Timothy was then the pastor at Ephesus. Normally a church will manifest a burden for souls if the pastor shows genuine evangelistic zeal. Any church is in serious trouble whose pastor and people do not live with a conviction of the truth of 2 Corinthians 5:20: "Now then we are ambassadors for Christ, as though God did beseech you by us: we pray you in Christ's stead, be ye reconciled to God."

Opportunities To Evangelize

1. The pulpit ministry is vital. ". . . It pleased God by the foolishness of preaching to save them that believe" (1 Cor. 1:21). A pastor must teach as well as evangelize. Both ministries may be effectually woven into the same message. A ministry that is all teaching and no evangelism will produce a dead, formal church. A ministry that is all evangelism and no teaching will produce a church that is impotent and easily deceived because it is not built up in the faith. Even its evangelism will fail.

2. The Sunday Bible school, vacation Bible school, summer camps and youth organizations are invaluable channels of evangelism in a local church. Teachers and leaders should be trained and constantly challenged in soul winning. They must not become bogged down in methodology or complacent over statistical progress.

3. House-to-house visitation is hard work, but it pays eternal dividends. The Lord has taught us to go out into the highways and byways

(Luke 14:23). It is reasonable to fish where the fish are, and to fish for men where the men are.

4. Hospital calling provides opportunities to reach people for Christ when they desperately need help and often are ready to listen to the Word.

5. Tract distribution has been honored of the Lord. It usually supplements personal soul winning in other forms, but our sovereign God often speaks in power to hearts through literature without oral ministry.

6. Street meetings have been very fruitful in some areas. They have come into ill repute and uselessness in other places where radicals in religion or politics have usurped the proverbial soap box for evil purposes. We need to use wisdom in seeking effective methods.

7. Radio and television have afforded unprecedented opportunities to reach vast numbers of people with the gospel. When such ministries have been wisely conducted, they have been used to win men to Christ. Great care needs to be exercised not to spend large sums of money on such work if it is not evidently within the Lord's will. This approach must never displace personal contact with people as we seek their souls.

8. Personal witnessing to neighbors, relatives and business and school associates is one of the most fruitful means of evangelizing people. Its basic weakness is the fact that too few Christians practice it!

However, no matter how many of the above and other methods are used, a church is neglecting one of its greatest evangelistic opportunities if it fails to hold special evangelistic meetings. God has given to certain men the gift of evangelism. Such men should be sought by churches to work with the pastor and people in special times of concentrated effort to reach men for Christ. The other efforts throughout the year will be enhanced by such special meetings. Some churches have at least two such series of meetings annually. More churches plan one series.

The busy schedules of our modern day have discouraged long evangelistic meetings. Formerly they extended for weeks, or indefinitely, until the Lord brought great conviction and many conversions. Now most of the meetings do not exceed two weeks. Frequently they are reduced to one week. This usually proves to be too short a time to accomplish any extensive or intensive work in the hearts of men. We urgently need such a burden upon our hearts to see men saved that we will put aside our own schedules and pleasures to accomplish more effective work for our Lord!

Problems Accompanying Evangelistic Efforts

1. We are prone to place the burden of the work upon an evangelist or an evangelistic team, then sit down and wait for results. This is not God's way.

2. Frequently evangelism is divorced from the local church. Union campaigns (in addition to other serious problems) have eclipsed the local church and also impersonalized its impact upon people. The campaign is usually held in a neutral location, such as a tent or public auditorium. The converts have not seen the local church, identified its people, nor felt the warmth of its fellowship. It is logical to expect that a smaller percentage of professions in such campaigns result in membership in Bible-preaching churches than when the local church conducts its own meetings. God established churches to carry on His work. Any methods that minimize the local church are at least second-best, and are probably unbiblical.

3. Union campaigns rarely avoid the serious evil of compromise on Biblical doctrines. Even when no liberal churches are involved, the evangelist and personal workers are faced with problems. What doctrines may be preached? Lest some be offended, the workers must be silent about immersion, eternal security, a sovereign God, the choice of a church home and many other things. Even though these restrictions are not written out, they are understood and practiced.

Many people today have been brainwashed with the concepts that everything worthwhile must be big; that doctrinal convictions must be forsaken in the interests of evangelism; that the only thing really important in Christian work is securing "commitments" to Christ; and that the end justifies the means. Not one of these things is true. We do not have to do evil that good may come. We do not have to disobey the Word of God to win souls! God will honor those who honor Him!

4. Ecumenical evangelism violates Biblical principles more than almost any evangelistic activity. It has two major areas of disobedience to God: it brings together God's people with unbelievers and apostates as yokefellows in God's service (the Bible strongly denounces such a practice); and it sends those who have made "commitments" to the "church of their choice," even though it is an apostate Protestant church, a Roman Catholic church or whatever. No warning is given of the false doctrines and principles of such groups. Ethically, no warning can be given, for the false and apostate leaders are on the platform, on the committees, in the inquiry room and active in the leadership. Thus the distinctions between truth and error are subtly removed from the minds of the masses of people because these distinctions are obscured

and virtually denied by the public cooperation of conservative and liberal church leaders.

Ecumenical evangelism, through the two characteristics mentioned above, has been one of the major forces that has accelerated the development of the apostate ecumenical church, in spite of the souls that have been saved in such meetings. It is not our purpose here to document the evils of ecumenical evangelism. Others have done this thoroughly. We simply warn in the light of the following Scriptures that such involvement is unbiblical. Read 2 John 9-11; Galatians 1:8, 9; 2 Corinthians 6:14—7:1; 2 Thessalonians 3:6, 14; 1 Timothy 1:19, 20; 1 Timothy 6:3-5; 2 Timothy 2:16-18; Romans 16:17.

Biblical Methods of Evangelism

There are sound and Biblical methods of evangelism that are effective and avoid the problems outlined above. God's people should follow such procedures and avoid the dangers that accompany human methods, which are too often characterized by expediency.

1. Pastor and people should pray and plan as God leads. *Determine dates* (perhaps for several years in advance in order to be able to secure evangelists). *Choose an evangelist* by church action. When the people are involved in the decision, there is an added sense of responsibility and participation. Decide on a man only after careful investigation as to doctrine, godliness, methods, finances, measure of cooperation with the pastor and church, and the testimony of other churches where he has ministered.

2. Continued prayer, both public and private, should also include prayer meetings in the homes, prayer lists and subsequently, pre-service prayer sessions. "Except the LORD build the house, they labour in vain that build it . . ." (Ps. 127:1).

3. Trained personal workers are essential in the life of any church and are vitally needed in evangelistic meetings. Hold training sessions in soul winning. Such a session may be conveniently arranged during the Sunday evening training hour or as a special class during the Sunday school hour.

4. An able, spiritual song leader and accompanist are vital needs. Early planning is necessary to secure good personnel. The church may have such individuals, or it may have to call them from elsewhere. If the evangelist is chosen first, he may have some suggestions.

5. An outstanding quartet or soloist will add appeal to the public and will contribute greatly to the spiritual impact of the meetings. A church must never lose sight of the fact, however, that the musical

program and other aspects of the meeting must be only supplemental to the preaching of the Word.

6. Faithful, capable ushers are a must. They are hosts to greet strangers and contribute to the sense of welcome and goodwill. They should be trained in how to seat people graciously, provide songbooks for all, take the offering efficiently and control heat and ventilation properly. (Be sure that a sufficient number of plates are available to enable the men to receive the offering quickly.)

7. An evangelistic service is not a money-raising event. Souls are the objective. The fewer offerings taken, the better the impression on the unsaved.

The expenses for advertising, workers, the evangelist's travel and living costs and other expenses should be known in advance. Some churches give this money in offerings before the evangelistic series or take it from their regular budget. Others have given the needed amount in the early days of the series and then taken no other such offerings.

Usually an evangelist is called on the basis of a free-will offering. This will be received at previously announced sessions, perhaps on two evenings a week.

8. Good tracts and other helpful literature should be secured in advance. A few Bibles may be needed for people coming from homes without Bibles. Decision cards should be prepared to keep an adequate record of decisions to enable proper follow-up.

9. The evangelist normally conducts the invitation. It should be clear and genuine and not based upon great emotional appeals. It should never be based on pressure or embarrassment. It should not, normally, be extended over a long period. No effort should be made to get great numbers forward for the sake of numbers or to build the reputation of the evangelist. By using a wide variety of appeals that may easily cause people to come, many hypocritical decisions have been made in order to avoid being conspicuous.

10. Be sure that a conveniently located inquiry room is prepared, equipped with chairs, well lighted and comfortable. It is preferable to deal with people in this situation, rather than in the noise of the auditorium after the service.

Great care should be exercised in leading people to a clear assurance of salvation. Prayerful patience, wise use of the Word and a genuine love of souls are essential at this point. No pressure or embarrassment should be permitted.

11. The follow-up work after an evangelistic series is as vital as the series itself. The fruit should be preserved. Contacts should be continued. Two areas are involved: instructing and helping new con-

verts; and seeking to win others who attended but made no decision, and those who are family members or friends of the newly saved. Too often this aspect of the work is neglected.

It is very good to have at least one friend who is specifically responsible for each convert. This person can do much to make the new babe in Christ feel wanted and at home in the church, Sunday school and social life of the church. Personal calls, an invitation to dinner, introductions to other friends, times for prayer and Bible study on a personal basis and the answering of questions will produce rapid growth in the new life.

The pastor's work in the follow-up is crucial. Every effort must be made to ground the converts in the Word and bring them quickly to baptism and church membership.

Instruction classes have been used in many churches with real profit. The pastor may prepare material for these classes, or it may be purchased.

12

The Missionary Program of the Church

THE CHURCH is a missionary organization. To it has been revealed the most wonderful message known to man. To it has been committed the most tremendous undertaking in human history. The enemies of this work are legion. The task involves: (1) the evangelizing of the whole world, including each generation of men as it moves swiftly across the stage of time; (2) evangelizing individuals speaking thousands of languages and dialects; (3) evangelizing with a message totally foreign to the thinking of all natural men; (4) the consecration of our own lives which, apart from His sustaining grace, are too fickle and selfish for such a colossal task; (5) undergoing the opposition of wicked spirits and Satan, who use force and the deception of every possible distraction of false religions and worldliness; (6) distances and ocean barriers to retard the work; and (7) a fallen creation under the curse with its dangers and diseases to challenge the stoutest hearts.

But God did not "suggest" that we go; He commanded it! People without Christ are not merely miserable; they are lost! The church must act and carry the gospel now, or betray our Lord Who placed this responsibility upon us.

In spite of the enemies that confront us, we need not hesitate or fear! Remember that He Who said, "Go," also said, ". . . Lo, I am with you alway, even unto the end of the world. Amen" (Matt. 28:19, 20). Through His Holy Spirit our hearts are stabilized and the hearts of others are opened to receive the Christ we preach. With the shield of faith, we quench the fiery darts of the wicked (Eph. 6:16). The battle is the Lord's, and He is infinitely greater than all the enemies. We are responsible to obey. He will provide the strength and the victory.

The missionary work must rest upon the churches. We are responsible as individuals to be consecrated to this task; but we are to be bound together in churches, according to God's plan. The Book of Acts makes it evident that the local church, not isolated individuals, was responsible to send out and sustain the missionaries. This responsibility cannot be shifted to missionary societies, even though they are an indispensable help to the churches.

The church must have a missionary burden or be disobedient to its Head. It dare not become self-centered or it will shrivel into impotence.

The Basis for Missions

Compassion for our fellowmen will produce a missionary church if we have the mind of Christ. "But when he saw the multitudes, he was moved with compassion on them, because they fainted, and were scattered abroad, as sheep having no shepherd. Then saith he . . . Pray ye therefore the Lord of the harvest, that he will send forth labourers into his harvest" (Matt. 9:36-38).

We know the satisfying ministry of Christ in our lives. Dare we withhold from the lost the good news of the gospel? There should be in our hearts a spontaneous desire to seek their deliverance from the bondage of sin in which we were once held. Any other attitude is crass selfishness. We do well to remember the words of the four lepers outside the starving city of Samaria after they had discovered the bounties of food in the deserted camp of the Syrians: "We do not well: this day is a day of good tidings, and we hold our peace . . ." (2 Kings 7:9).

Obedience to the forthright commands of our Lord is the primary basis of all missionary work. ". . . Ye shall be witnesses unto me both in Jerusalem, and in all Judaea, and in Samaria, and unto the uttermost part of the earth" (Acts 1:8). To the church at Corinth, it was written that He "hath given to us the ministry of reconciliation. . . . Now then we are ambassadors for Christ . . ." (2 Cor. 5:18-21).

The infant church, moved by compassion and obedience, flamed with missionary zeal so that the known world was evangelized in that day (Acts 8:4; Rom. 10:18), even though it required a severe persecution to arouse them from their ease and complacency (Acts 8:1-3). May we be faithful without having to be prodded by persecution!

The Objective of Missions

Evangelism.   Our basic responsibility is evangelism, the confronting of each soul with the fact of his desperate need as a sinner, the impending judgment of God upon him, and the good news of Christ's death and resurrection for his personal salvation. Our responsibility is to preach this Christ, but our consuming burden is to see men respond and trust Christ unto eternal life. We cannot adequately preach the gospel as an obligation; it must be accompanied with a passion for the souls of men.

Indigenous churches.   The establishing of indigenous churches is a crucial part of our missionary objective. An indigenous church is one that is self-governing, self-supporting and self-propagating. We believe that now, as in New Testament times, men won to Christ in any community should organize a local church. This church is to elect its own officers, conduct its own business, reach its own decisions. It is not to be governed by the missionary, and he is not to be its pastor. As in apostolic days, these infant churches will need counsel and guidance at the beginning; but this should be aimed at establishing the church on its own initiative at the earliest possible moment. This new church is to be responsible to provide its own building and support its own pastor, and not to be subsidized from other lands. Temporary help of one church by another may be wise and Christian, but even this must be done cautiously lest the church fail to trust the Lord and undertake its own responsibilities. The new church is also to be self-propagating by sending out evangelists and missionaries to others so that more souls may be won and established in local churches.

If pressed vigorously and wisely, this method will enable us to grow with amazing rapidity to the glory of Christ. It was so in apostolic times. Today, we have become too complacent in many ways!

Training nationals.   The training of national Christians won in our missionary work is another crucial part of our objective. In some lands this involves the development of a written language and, of course, the translation of the Word into that language. Converts must then learn to read and then to study and preach that Word. It is slow, tedious work. It requires the dedicated services of our finest young people. It justifies the sacrificial giving of our churches. It results in a strong local church that will serve the Lord and evangelize that area as no foreign missionary can ever do. It assures a permanent testimony even if the missionaries are driven out of the land.

Other ministries.   Medical, educational, charitable and other institutional aspects of missionary work may be used to good advantage in many places, but only if evangelism is the primary objective and these things are subordinated as a means to that end. This will be discussed more under dangers of missions. In some lands those approaches are now required by the governments before missionaries can enter.

The Coordination of Missions

The church, the school and the mission agency, by coordinating their efforts, can accomplish the most effective missionary work with the church as the responsible center of this activity—the captain of this team.

In the church people are saved, nurtured and dedicated to His service. From the church they go forth to serve. To the church they look for support of all kinds; and to the church they return to report and give an account.

The school is established, essentially as an arm of the church, to provide the intensive training in the Word and in Biblical methods of procedure. The church is responsible to guide its prospective workers to schools that teach the whole counsel of God. As a basic principle, Baptist churches desiring to establish sound Baptist missionary activities in other lands should train their missionaries in Baptist schools. Thank God for our fine missionaries who have gone out from other schools. But many problems have arisen needlessly because workers were not trained to know what Baptists believe and how they operate. (Furthermore, we could weep over many of our fine young people who have been lost to our work as a result of their attendance at other schools.) Most other denominations practice the policy of training their own young people going into leadership, but some Baptists become very critical when it is suggested that Baptists follow this logical procedure. They seem to feel this is some new idea. Let us examine carefully the training centers for our youth. They deserve to be taught the whole truth in the most effective manner. Our own schools are decisive links in the chain of missionary responsibilities.

The missionary agency is also an arm of the churches, practically providing technical experience and leadership in assisting the churches to send out their missionaries. There are involved problems with foreign governments, field methods and financing which are greatly reduced in this way, thus relieving the churches of needless research, expense and trouble.

The missionary agency, society or association also simplifies the coordination of finances from many small churches for the support of missionaries.

There must be a careful, gracious cooperation, for the missionary agency must not eclipse the personal relationship of the missionary to the church, or churches, sending him out. However, the churches must give a maximum of cooperation to the mission in the interests of efficient placement of missionaries, handling of finances for the missionaries and determining of field policies.

The missionary must also sense the teamwork between the church and mission, as well as between himself and his fellow missionaries, and seek prayerfully to be pliable to the Lord's direction through these other people of God, as well as to Him personally.

The Program of Missions

The church's missionary program may well include a missionary committee. Often the deacons and pastor form this committee; or it may be enlarged by the election of other members. It is responsible to plan and suggest improvement in the church's mission work, to examine any prospective missionaries, recommend financial responsibilities to the church, maintain contact with and help the church's missionaries as much as possible and fulfill other such duties. Decisions, of course, must rest with the church.

The ladies' missionary society to sew and provide other such help for the missionaries is a commendable part of the program.

An all-church missionary society is most desirable, however. This should include all members of the church in an active group. Some churches following this plan meet one evening a month for a simple fellowship supper. This affords needed social fellowship and enables many to come who could not do so otherwise. Promptly after supper, a planned program of study is undertaken. Children, young people and adults meet in separate groups under capable teachers to study our mission agencies, their various fields, practices and problems, as well as the individual missionaries and their needs. (The mission agencies will be glad to furnish needed literature for this study.) This period is basically informational. Immediately following, an inspirational service is held, with a challenging missionary message and a missionary offering. Prayer is also an essential part of such a meeting, even though it is not the primary objective of this session.

If the supper is held from 6:00 to 6:45 and the class from 6:45 to 7:30, the entire evening may be concluded by 8:30—early enough so the children may attend.

Such a program relates the mission responsibilities to men and women, young and old, in a proper way. The women's mission group, meeting midway between these sessions, will supplement this profitably.

The pastor's enthusiastic leadership is vital to the church's mission program.

The missionaries must be kept before the church for prayer. Part of the church bulletin can sometimes be devoted to excerpts from their letters or prayer requests for them. Some churches publish in monthly mimeographed folders the letters from their missionaries, so that all the church may be kept informed.

Letters should be sent regularly to the missionaries. The pastor should not be responsible for all this. A missionary committee may assign someone (or secure volunteers) to write each week.

Tape recorders are being used effectively to send personal messages to the missionaries and to receive from them live reports on the work being done.

Missionary conferences may be a means of stirring new life in a local church. Messages, panels, forums, films and personal conferences with missionaries fresh from fields of active service will bring a new challenge to any church! Our mission agencies will be happy to assist in setting up such a conference.

Boxes of supplies, birthday gifts, Christmas gifts and other such encouragements can be sent profitably to many missionaries. However, either the missionary or the mission should be consulted first. In some countries import duty may cost the missionary more than the worth of the gifts. Proper methods of wrapping and shipping should be determined, as well as what gifts are really needed and what ones will "survive" shipment to each country.

Furloughs are a vital part of missionary work. A missionary must have adequate rest from the pressure of duties and adverse climates. He must renew his contacts at home for prayer and support. He may at this time be a great blessing to the church. Obviously, his support should continue. Help should be provided in securing adequate housing for the furlough. Acts 14:27 and 28 form an interesting conclusion to Paul's missionary journey.

The Dangers of Missions

History has demonstrated that we often lose our first love, and work that was started well degenerates into a mere form. Some missions that were founded by men with sound doctrine and a passion for souls are now directed by others as mere social service agencies. Because the physical need is evident, human compassion may prevail over the spiritual burden. Thus, medical and educational units of the mission take the primary place and gradually become the objective, instead of merely a means to reach men's souls.

We need to pray earnestly for our missionaries and to keep in close touch with policies and attitudes to guard against such deterioration.

Another missionary danger faced by our churches is the giving of money and other support to missions that are unworthy. Unfortunately, some men can give glowing reports without having any real mission work in progress. It is safe to give to our established missions with responsible boards. Real care should be exercised in order that we may be faithful stewards.

Satanic attacks upon the bodies and minds of missionaries are a constant danger. He has not been able to corrupt our doctrine, but he is striving to prevent its proclamation. We must surround our missionaries with believing prayer and assure them of our understanding and love.

13

The Finances of the Church

ACCURATE, BUSINESSLIKE methods of handling money greatly enhance the testimony of a church. A community loses respect for a church that is careless or incompetent about financial matters. Furthermore, thorough, responsible officers and methods will increase the income of a church because of greater confidence on the part of the donors.

A careful review of finances from time to time is a wholesome practice for any church.

A Financial Checklist

Officers.   Financial officers must be spiritual, honest and reputable people. In addition, they must know how to handle money properly and how to keep clear, accurate records. Money must be protected against loss or theft. A good insurance man can give information on the bonding of those handling the funds. Exact records protect against confusion as to funds in which the money belongs. Records must be kept up-to-date on both receipts and disbursements. These should show all monies received, where and when they were expended, and what balances are on hand in each fund.

Reports.   Reports should be made to the church at least quarterly by both the financial secretary and the treasurer. These reports should include details, not merely balances. Accurate information will encourage giving. The members of the church are entitled to know what is being done with the money they give. Copies of reports should be available for each member. Officers should be prepared to answer questions concerning details.

Deposits.   All funds should be deposited promptly in a bank. Money kept in homes or churches is subject to loss or theft. Proper, locked money bags may be secured. (See your bank.) Many churches use these and place the money in the night deposit vault of the bank promptly after the service.

Payments.   All bills should be paid by check. In no other way can the church be protected properly. Nothing should be paid in cash. Checks form good protection as receipts and eliminate many problems over errors in billing the church. No adequate audit can be made of the church accounts unless all bills are paid by check.

Purchases.   Purchases in the name of the church must be approved by the church or by the trustees. There must be official authorization for the expenditure of funds. Some items are routine, such as salaries previously determined by vote of the church, or repairs and improvements done on contracts approved by the church. These and other items, such as supplies, equipment and utilities, should be approved by the trustees before payment is made. Such approval protects both the treasurer and the church.

Audit.   The church books should be audited annually by a professional auditor or by a competent committee within the membership. This does not express distrust of the officers. All thoughtful, honest officers will welcome, if not insist upon, an audit. Such action has at least four major benefits.

1. It protects the reputation of the financial officers against suspicion or gossip.

2. It protects the officers against temptation (which may come upon anyone), since they know that they must give an accounting.

3. It insures the confidence of the members in the soundness of the financial policies of the church.

4. It helps to improve methods of bookkeeping and reporting.

Honesty.   Scrupulous honesty must be followed in all details. At least two people should count the offering and keep a permanent record before turning the funds over to the financial secretary, who keeps the official records of monies received. The financial secretary should deposit the money promptly and deliver immediately to the treasurer the deposit slip and a record of the amount to go to each fund.

When special offerings are taken, the money received must be used for the announced purpose. Diversion of such funds to other objectives is dishonest.

Offerings.   Normally it is advisable to bring the offerings back to the front of the church and count the money following the meeting. It is unfair to officers to keep them out of the services regularly. Furthermore, it creates an unwholesome impression of disinterest on their part in the ministry of the Word.

Envelopes.   Numbered church envelopes are proper. They have at least two distinct advantages.

1. They enable individuals to give without other identification and still obtain an official receipt for tax purposes. This is very important, for while we are to be honest in the payment of all taxes due, it is foolish to pay in excess of this amount. Information concerning these envelopes should be absolutely confidential. Only the financial secretary should have access to the information concerning the individual giving. This must not be divulged in whole or in part to the pastor or anyone else.

2. These envelopes enable people to give more systematically, which is a help to both them and the church.

Giving.   It scarcely needs to be said that all giving should be free and voluntary. No spiritual work can prosper adequately if financed by suppers, bazaars, raffles or community drives for funds.

Giving should be systematic, proportionate and joyful. Those who give less than the tithe rob both themselves and the Lord. We are here discussing the church's responsibilities, not the individual's, so this point is not enlarged.

Insurance.   The church's financial responsibility is not complete without careful attention concerning insurance upon buildings and equipment. Every church is sovereign in all such decisions. However, it is certainly the general conviction that substantial insurance should be carried. While we commit our lives and all that we have unto the Lord, it is evident from the great number of church fires that He is not always pleased to prevent such fires. When a building burns without insurance, the news does not commend the church to its members or to the community as a whole. The financial future of the church is in jeopardy in such a case.

Careful, periodic review of insurance programs is essential. Values change greatly in these inflationary periods. Professional counsel on these matters can prove very profitable to a church. We are stewards of God over all we possess, and someday we must give an account to Him.

A portion in Ezra 8:24-34 is a sound lesson in careful stewardship. The gold and silver belonging to God were carefully weighed, counted and committed into the hands of chosen men.

14

Some Problems
of the Church

IT SEEMS THAT PROBLEMS are perennial for everyone! Often we feel that we have more than our share! But ". . . God is faithful, who will not suffer you to be tempted above that ye are able; but will with the temptation also make a way to escape, that ye may be able to bear it" (1 Cor. 10:13).

All our churches have problems. It is wholesome to recognize their reality and to honestly seek their solution. The acknowledgment and analysis of our problems are major strides in eliminating them.

May we, as adults, be very frank with ourselves as we face these things. We may find that we have contributed more to the problems than we have realized. We may also find that we have done far less than we could have done to help the pastor, the deacons and our other leaders in dealing with these things successfully.

Usually the major quarrels that divide churches, on other than doctrinal issues, stem out of very simple things. Some jealousy between two classes, a misunderstanding within the choir, or some trivial matter in a young people's meeting may be enough for the flesh and the Devil to team up to ruin the testimony of a church for years, although neither side of the dispute had any idea of starting such a conflict. If we can sensibly recognize our weaknesses and deal with them, we may, through His gracious leadership, avoid those times of heartache that otherwise might attack us.

Friendliness Versus Cliques

A clique is described in the dictionary as a small set that is snobbish or exclusive. Many churches have such groups. Sometimes they center in an ambitious leader, or in some class, or in a "political" group within the church, one that is opposed to the pastor or to the position of the church. Most frequently they result from a selfish, complacent attitude that emphasizes social activity and tragically lacks any burden for souls.

Occasionally such situations may require disciplinary action. More frequently they can be conquered by prayer and forthright friend-liness by the rest of the church members. Often they are taken too seriously. Too much attention flatters such people like spoiled chil-dren, for they have a carnal attitude.

Some churches suffer badly from cliques. However, the situation is rarely as serious and damaging as the agitation concerning the sup-posed clique! The more the situation is discussed, the more self-conscious all parties become. Let us ask the Lord to help us forget ourselves and pray for those who seem self-centered. The results will be encouraging!

I have observed through the years that those who complain the most that a church is unfriendly are the first to rush out after a meeting before anyone can be friendly. The Word says that if we would have friends, we must be friendly (Prov. 18:24). If we are willing to help others instead of pitying ourselves, willing to work instead of complain-ing, smile instead of scowling, pray instead of criticizing, forgive in-stead of accusing, we shall find a friendly church. The supposed cliques will disappear amazingly!

Often a pastor is censured for being more friendly with some than with others, and a party spirit is developed. We should remember that a pastor has no pastor and, without being a respecter of persons, he may really need some special friends. The Lord Jesus had some very special friends in Bethany. I heard one pastor who was being criticized say, "I am happy to go into any home or group in our church where I'm invited." The critics would be silenced if they would venture a cordial, "How about having dinner with us tonight, Pastor?"

Class activities and competition are necessary and wholesome, but they can be overdone until the groups become a series of little churches within a church. Departmentalizing can be carried to an extreme. There is an urgent need for more *church* functions, for both social fellowship and spiritual ministry. All the members of a church need to know each other, pray for each other and work with each other at a common task. The common task may be an intensive house-to-house visitation campaign, an evangelistic effort, painting or remodeling the church building or parsonage. Friendliness will bloom in the midst of the challenge for teamwork.

Irreverence

This is a real problem in many of our churches! However, we need to beware of admiring the quiet formalism of some groups, for often it is not reverence but the "hush of death." Reverence is not produced by (though it may accompany) soft music, stained-glass windows and thick rugs! True reverence is produced by the consciousness of and delight in the presence of God. Joy and gladness are not irreverent unless they are carnal levity. Read Psalm 100.

Several very common but unnecessary things distract from proper reverence in many of our churches.

Poorly planned and unorganized services.   They present too many distractions with delays, mistakes or omissions in the meeting. Such a situation also leaves the impression (which may be too true!) that the service was not considered to be of sufficient importance to be prepared adequately. These problems usually relate to announcements that have not been turned in properly; to misunderstandings in relation to choirs, accompanists, ushers, etc. These reactions make it difficult for the people to concentrate in worship.

Undisciplined children.   Children who are allowed to run up and down the aisles to fountains and rest rooms certainly distract in a serious way. Proper forethought on the part of parents or teachers, coupled with some firm discipline, can quickly remove this problem. It may also help to have the teachers in the classes teach and challenge the children. With the smaller ones, of course, the matter needs to be brought to the attention of the parents.

Parents are to be admired and commended when they bring their families to church. Other people should learn to rejoice in this, and not be distracted by normal noises and movements of small children. But babies who cry loudly or persistently should be taken out. Adequate nurseries and mothers' rooms are helpful where they can be provided.

Children are sometimes allowed to run and make excessive commotion in auditoriums or prayer rooms, even when people are talking and dealing with souls. We do not consider a church building to be the temple—our bodies are that. But it is dedicated to a holy purpose, and respect and reverence for the Lord as we meet in that building are to be exercised.

Laughing and careless talk.   Laughing and talking carelessly of temporal things are poor preparation for a worship service. There is so much clatter in some churches as the pastor seeks to open the service that it can scarcely be drowned by a good organ! There seems to be little anticipation of meeting the Lord. If we knew that any moment the Lord Jesus would step onto the platform, there would be a hushed expectancy. But if we are met in His name, He says, ". . . There am I in the midst of them" (Matt. 18:20).

Carnal young people.   A few obviously carnal young people who gather in balconies or rear seats and manifest attitudes varying from indifference to defiance are one of the greatest causes of irreverence. Their activities vary from talking and note-writing to open, sensual necking. Sometimes they belong to the church and may be from some of the finest families in the church. As parents, we ought not to be so idealistic as to suppose that our children can do no wrong. This is a problem that should receive the wholehearted and prayerful cooperation of parents, deacons and pastor. The church that rebukes this practice may lose a few people (2 Tim. 4:2). The church that does not will lose its testimony! Love and patience must be manifested—but not softness nor indulgence.

I have spoken in hundreds of churches in the past few years, and the above situation is serious. However, in defense of a host of fine, spiritual young people in our churches across the land, let it be said that it is not typical. Some of the most consecrated, earnest members of our Bible-preaching Baptist churches are young people who have a real testimony for Christ!

Indifference

This point is not written with any pessimism or sense of defeatism. A host of God's people are burdened for souls, alert for opportunities to serve and generous in their stewardship to the point of sacrifice. But we are all painfully aware of another host—a very large host—of people with names on the rolls of Bible-preaching churches, who are careless in attendance, unwilling to accept any responsibility and who have never been heard to pray or to witness.

The Lord is the only One Who knows, but in all probability many of these indifferent souls have never been saved. Preaching, praying and personal work should be directed faithfully toward these people. We ought never to take their attitude for granted. It is not normal. Something is critically wrong with anyone who professes to trust the Savior Who suffered the anguish of Calvary, and died as his Substitute, and who yet ignores and disobeys that Savior. Nothing but sin can make people that ungrateful.

The Word teaches, however, that even saved people can become carnal in their walk (1 Cor. 3:1-4). During these days of easy money and lush prosperity, carnality is a more evident enemy of our souls. The world creeps in with its threefold delusion: "For all that is in the world, the lust of the flesh, and the lust of the eyes, and the pride of life, is not of the Father, but is of the world" (1 John 2:16). "But they that will be rich fall into temptation and a snare. . . . For the love of money is the root of all evil: which while some coveted after, they have erred from the faith, and pierced themselves through with many sorrows" (1 Tim. 6:9, 10).

One cannot serve God and mammon (Matt. 6:24). The effort always ends in spiritual disaster. First Peter 2:11 supplies invaluable counsel: "Dearly beloved, I beseech you as strangers and pilgrims, abstain from fleshly lusts, which war against the soul." Romans 6 and Galatians 2:20 furnish the method of victory. We are crucified with Christ! He does live in us! How we should praise Him for that!

A carnal self-life and profession without salvation are two of the most common and deadly causes of indifference among professing Christians. You could name many others. Christ is the answer to each one. Let us so live and so preach Christ before those who are cold that they may be made to hunger after the reality with which our hearts are satisfied in Him!

Finances

The old "oyster supper" type of church financing is very uncommon today. Praise the Lord for churches that shun such carnal methods because of conviction. God does have a way of financing His work, but it is not by bazaars and suppers! Regular, systematic and proportionate giving from joyful hearts honors the Lord and abundantly sustains His work. This is plainly commanded in such portions as 1 Corinthians 16:2: "Upon the first day of the week . . . as God has prospered. . . ." Second Corinthians 8 sets forth many other details. Certainly under grace we ought to give more joyfully and more bountifully than the tithe required under the old law!

While our churches have undertaken many new financial responsibilities and the totals sound impressive, actually we should be ashamed! Few churches receive more than fifty cents per day per member! You don't believe it? Check your own church! Some churches with "clean" church rolls do better, but not many others. When we consider what we spend on mere luxuries of life, let us not talk about having reached our limit of missionary giving. It is true that a group in each church is giving sacrificially. The indifferent host that we discussed before accounts for this tragic average. May the Lord arouse all of us to our urgent obligation to be faithful stewards of all we have.

The other basic problem results from the common practice of scattering the giving in an unscriptural manner. The local church is established by God. It is responsible to propagate the gospel, edify the saints and administer the Lord's work. Because many of the Lord's people have not seen the importance of the local church in God's program, they have scattered their giving into all manner of channels, many of which are unworthy, unnecessary or, at best, secondary to the work of the church. This "bleeds" vitally needed support from the local church and its missionary program until it cannot do the job it should.

Let us review our church covenant to which we agreed when we joined the church. Among other things, it states: "We purpose, therefore, by the aid of the Holy Spirit . . . to contribute cheerfully and regularly, as God has prospered us, to the support of the ministry, the expenses of the church, the relief of the poor, and the spread of the gospel throughout all nations."

In the light of God's Word, let us examine prayerfully our own individual practices of giving, as well as the voluntary agreement of the covenant above. If we do so honestly, perhaps the envelopes we put into the plate in the weeks ahead will be thicker!

The Church and the Community

The testimony of a church centers in its pulpit ministry, but this is adorned or marred by many other things.

The property of the church is a real factor in molding the attitude of the community toward a church. Some needed repairs, a good coat of paint and some landscaping often overcome much bias. Progress and growth have aroused the interest of many who were indifferent.

Business methods are vital to the church's ministry. Efficient officers who capably represent the church at the bank and the business houses; bills that are paid on time; reports that are accurate and comprehensive; and sound business procedure in the conduct of all church affairs—these team up to leave a very favorable impression on the community, especially among professional people who are so often neglected and unreached for Christ.

Friendliness toward the community in which we witness is a vital factor in our successful winning of men. Since we cannot be friendly with worldly and sinful practices and cannot therefore simply be "good mixers" in many aspects of community life, it becomes necessary to have special wisdom and grace to prove our friendliness to the people, and our concern for them, without becoming involved in many of their activities. There are places where we can help without compromise, and we should do so heartily. Christ was not a recluse. He ate with publicans and sinners; but He went to minister to them, not to fellowship with their sin! Only the overflowing love of Christ within us can enable us to withstand the world around us without seeming to be proud and pharisaical, or, on the other hand, to manifest our friendliness to those in the world without softening our convictions toward their sin.

This friendliness, so vital to our testimony, needs to be evident in the church as well as to our neighbors. The responsibility rests upon each member. Thoughtful, gracious, capable ushers are vital in this matter. They serve as hosts to guests as they arrive. First impressions are important!

Worldliness

One of the greatest problems a church can face is worldliness and sin in the lives of members. Whether in the pastor, officers or other members, this problem must be dealt with. If sin is indulged, the Holy Spirit is grieved and the church is powerless. The members are discouraged, babes in Christ are caused to stumble, the unsaved turn away from the church disgusted, and the Devil rejoices.

To prevent such a problem, the church needs a godly pastor who will be an example to all, and whose strong, Biblical ministry will expose and rebuke sin, as well as edify the believers.

The church must also exercise care in receiving into membership only those who are born again and are committed to honor the Lord. A desire to be big at any cost will destroy the purity of the church.

The Bible uses strong language in rebuking worldliness: ". . . Be not conformed to this world: but be ye transformed . . ." (Rom. 12:2). "Ye adulterers and adulteresses, know ye not that the friendship of the world is enmity with God? whosoever therefore will be a friend of the world is the enemy of God" (James 4:4).

The church must exercise patience and grace toward all, but this must not become indulgence of sin. Biblical discipline must be exercised without respect of persons toward the unrepentant who continue in their sins if the church is to follow her Lord and have an effective ministry. (See chapter 8.)

Young People

We draw this chapter to a close with a few observations which we believe will help in attracting and holding young people in our churches.

It is neither necessary nor desirable to resort to sensationalism nor worldly methods to win youth. They need honest answers to their flood of questions about God, the world around them, themselves and their own future. But these questions will not be asked freely until someone has demonstrated a personal interest and has gained their confidence. This takes time, patience and the love of Christ; but it pays infinite dividends.

Our young people respond to the challenge of the difficult. We have often spoiled them by trying to make the Christian life too soft and easy. Obviously they, as we, find it easier to live a life of compromise; but it is not a life of peace or satisfaction. A life sold out to Christ and His service is worth the world, and it costs just that!

They need social fellowship in our church activities. But they need even more a full program of spiritual activities, varying from a youth choir to a street meeting; from planning and conducting their own youth meetings to visitation and soul winning among their unsaved friends.

Leadership is vital. In many cases, the pastor may well invest his time in this ministry. Some churches can afford to secure a trained youth worker to focus attention on this very fruitful work. Some churches have very capable leaders within the membership. But keep in mind that the leader should be a member who is in full and hearty agreement with the church, its teaching and its pastor.

Conclusion

The Lord has promised wisdom to those who ask Him (James 1:5). Let us ask with confidence. We are confronted daily in the Lord's work with responsibilities and problems that are beyond human wisdom. It is blessed to know we can commit our way unto the Lord, trust also in Him, and He will bring it to pass (Ps. 37:5).

15

The Fellowship
of the Church

IT IS GOOD and pleasant for brethren to dwell together in unity! David compared it to the fragrance of the precious ointment that was poured upon the head of the high priest, and to the refreshing of the dew upon the mountains of Zion. This fragrance and refreshing should be ours, and they will be if we learn the reality of true, spiritual fellowship.

The Lord purposed for us the encouragement of fellowship. He commands that we should not forsake the company of His people (Heb. 10:25). Our communion with each other and with the Lord is obviously His purpose as outlined in 1 John 1. No man can be as "good a Christian" without the fellowship of a local church, regardless of the arguments presented by some who seek to excuse their absence from the house of God. We all urgently need the fragrance and the refreshing that are afforded in such communion!

Psalm 133:1 indicates that this fellowship is dependent upon two things: *First,* a common nature. We are to be brethren, born of one Father. *Second,* a common purpose. There must be unity instead of conflict, opposition or suspicion.

Fellowship Within the Local Church

Meaning of fellowship.   The meaning of fellowship is significant. One of the basic meanings of *fellow* is "a peer or an equal." Thus *fellowship* indicates the communion or companionship of peers or equals. This equality may not characterize all the features of those involved, but must be true of the areas vital to the basis of the fellowship. Even in the companionship of men in temporal things this is true. Music fans gather together because of an intense mutual interest in music. Golf enthusiasts gather at clubhouses and golf courses with their interest centered in the successes and failures that relate to a little white ball.

The fellowship in spiritual and heavenly things spans all the differences that may be common to natural life and brings into unity all believers in Christ. The rich and the poor, the cultured and the unlearned, the master and the servant—all find a new unity and equality that are fragrant and refreshing!

Basis of fellowship.   The basis of fellowship in the church is widely misunderstood even by many within the church. A basic critical error known as the "universal fatherhood of God and the universal brotherhood of man" is common today. On the strength of this false teaching, many believe that all men should be welcomed into our churches regardless of any experience of new birth. Such teaching is a complete repudiation of the Word of God which reveals that there are two families in this world, one born of Adam and the other of Christ; and that the one, therefore, is flesh and the other Spirit (1 Cor. 15:45-48; John 3:6, 7). The Word is clear that all of us by nature are the children of wrath (Eph. 2:3). When the Christ-rejecting Pharisees sought to persuade the Lord that God was their Father, He declared: "If God were your Father, ye would love me. . . . Ye are of your father the devil. . . . He that is of God heareth God's words: ye therefore hear them not, because ye are not of God" (John 8:42-47).

This twofold division within the human race is clearly shown in the words of John 3:18: "He that believeth on him is not condemned: but he that believeth not is condemned already, because he hath not believed. . . ." Men are either saved or lost, and there is no basis for fellowship between the two groups! ". . . What fellowship hath righteousness with unrighteousness? and what communion hath light with darkness? And what concord hath Christ with Belial? or what part hath he that believeth with an infidel?" (2 Cor. 6:14, 15).

The only basis of Christian fellowship is Christ! ". . . Our fellowship is with the Father, and with his Son Jesus Christ" (1 John 1:3). John writes in the same verse: "That which we have seen and heard [the incarnate Christ] declare we unto you, that ye also may have fellowship with us. . . ." Apart from the true Christ, real fellowship is impossible.

Obedience as well as faith is essential to our communion with each other. "But if we walk in the light, as he is in the light, we have fellowship one with another . . ." (1 John 1:7). The blessings of brethren dwelling together in unity are dependent therefore upon truth, believed and obeyed, and not upon compromise or mere sentimentality.

Methods of fellowship.   The methods of fellowship are numerous and may vary according to local conditions, but the principles are the same.

Real fellowship is enjoyed in the mutual study, discussion and proclamation of the Word of God. This may be found in the regular Sunday services of our church, in our Sunday school class and the midweek prayer meeting, providing that we come for that purpose. If we assemble with bitterness, jealousy or pride in our hearts, the act of fellowship is a mere pretense; and we go away complaining about the ministry, the minister and the people. Almost invariably such reactions are due to causes within ourselves that make impossible the fellowship with the people or with the Lord. But when our lives are clean and Spirit-filled, the very reading of the Word of God, the testimony of the humblest saint or the tearful prayer of some burdened soul knits our hearts to each other in a true spiritual fellowship that is more blessed than any relationship this world has to offer.

Fellowship is found in many places outside of formal meetings. The mutual brotherly love that finds expression in a flood of greetings and sympathy to those who suffer or sorrow; the food and the help that flow into a home when the mother is ill; those sacrificial gifts that are given to some brother in a crisis; the daily intercession for one another in our family prayers; the mutual rejoicing as our children and our neighbors confess our Lord Jesus—in these and scores of other ways, Christian fellowship between the members of a local church is a heartwarming and blessed experience. Obviously, the ministry of love and kindness goes beyond the borders of our own church, but there we have special privileges and responsibilities.

Fellowship may also be found in the social contacts with our brethren in Christ if we are walking in the Spirit. We should have a mutual love for each other and a mutual opposition to sin and the world that sanctify all our conduct and conversations. Some of the sweetest fellowship that can be experienced is enjoyed around a table with friends, long after the food is gone, as we talk of our joys and sorrows, our experiences in Christ and the glorious truths of His Word.

Dangers of fellowship.   The dangers of fellowship exist only when that fellowship is polluted with carnality. The social activities will be carried to excess and then move toward worldliness, eclipsing the spiritual life of the church. Wrong attitudes toward each other, even sensuality, can flourish in these conditions. Respect of persons will develop little cliques that ruin fellowship. Gossip will displace God, and selfishness will displace sacrifice. The fact of fellowship will have gone even while the form of it remains.

The cure for this danger is not the elimination of the fellowship, nor even the social contacts where we can enjoy real fellowship. Sin can flourish in a monastery. We shall not pollute our communion with each other if we learn the basic spiritual principle given in 1 Corinthians 10:31, "Whether therefore ye eat, or drink, or whatsoever ye do, do all to the glory of God."

Fellowship Beyond the Local Church

This is a topic that has tremendous significance in this day when the philosophy of the world and of the professing church is union (with or without unity!). One-world government and one-world church comprise the rosy concept of the dreamers of our day. Our churches, therefore, must exercise every caution to keep their Biblical balance. We must not be pushed off the beam of God's will to the left into ecumenism (one-world church), or off to the right into isolationism. God commands *unity of the faith* but *not a union of faiths.*

We recognize the sovereign right of each individual church to determine, under God, the extent and the direction of its fellowship beyond its own boundaries. We would claim our own liberties, however, to examine and discuss in the light of the Word the principles that are involved.

Forbidden areas of fellowship.

1. With the unsaved. While fellowship with the unsaved is forbidden, this does not mean isolation from them. We are to do good unto all men and we are to preach the gospel to every creature. The Lord Jesus Himself ate with publicans and sinners and wept over the shepherdless multitudes. But He went to the unsaved to minister to them; He did not go with them as companions.

Clear, positive commands of Scripture establish this point.

> Whosoever transgresseth, and abideth not in the doctrine of Christ, hath not God. He that abideth in the doctrine of Christ, he hath both the Father and the Son. If there come any unto you, and bring not this doctrine, receive him not into your house, neither bid him God speed: For he that biddeth him God speed is partaker of his evil deeds (2 John 9-11).
>
> Be ye not unequally yoked together with unbelievers: for what fellowship hath righteousness with unrighteousness? and what communion hath light with darkness? And what concord hath Christ with Belial? or what part hath he that believeth with an infidel? And what agreement hath the temple of God with idols? . . . Wherefore come out from among them, and be ye separate, saith the Lord, and touch not the unclean thing . . . (2 Cor. 6:14-18).

Certainly these and many parallel portions make clear that, as children of God, we have no right to join in any spiritual activity with those who reject our Lord Jesus. This forbids our praying with them as fellow-worshipers (even though we pray for them and witness to them) and forbids our belonging to the same churches with them, cooperating in union services with them or sponsoring any spiritual activity with them. No sentimentality nor sense of expediency will justify these practices which are so definitely forbidden in the Word of God.

Two prepositions used in the Scripture help to clarify the relationship we are to maintain with unbelievers. We are commanded to preach the gospel *to* every creature (Mark 16:15). But we are not to have fellowship *with* the unfruitful works of darkness (Eph. 5:11). We are not to be isolationists. We are to *go to* all men with God's message. But we are not to *go with* them in companionship, for this involves disobedience, defilement and defeat. We must examine our relationship to men without Christ. Are we going *to* them or *with* them?

2. With brethren in sin. We frequently hear the assertion: "I believe we should have unrestricted fellowship with all who profess faith in Christ." The Word of God denies this. Praise God that in Glory we shall have unrestricted and unending fellowship with all the redeemed! In the meantime certain things prevent us from enjoying that relationship now. Several portions of God's Word make this clear.

A man described in 1 Corinthians 5 had fallen into terrible moral sin, but the apostle Paul did not deny his salvation (vv. 5, 11; 2 Cor. 2:6-8). He did command: "But now I have written unto you not to keep company, if any man that is called a *brother* be a fornicator, or covetous, or an idolater, or a railer, or a drunkard, or an extortioner; with such an one no not to eat. . . . *Put away* from among yourselves that wicked person" (1 Cor. 5:11, 13). Note in the context, beginning with verse 9, that the apostle is far more rigid concerning our contact with one called a brother who is in sin than with men of the world. Contact with the brother in sin will be construed as fellowship and indulgence of his sin, while in contacting the unregenerate there is no basis for fellowship or indulgence. We are merely witnesses to them. This Biblical principle is crucial to the doctrine of separation. It is therefore untrue that we are to have unrestricted fellowship with all who profess faith in Christ.

Paul seems to be speaking of carnal Christians within the company in Romans 16:17 (for he says elsewhere that we are not to judge those on the outside, but those within): ". . . *Mark them* which cause divisions and offences contrary to the doctrine which ye have learned; and *avoid them.*" The same thought is set forth in Titus 3:10: "A man that is an heretick [literally, a factious man, or a man who causes factions, contentions and strife] after the first and second admonition *reject.*"

Nothing could more clearly affirm the need of refusing fellowship with some brethren than 2 Thessalonians 3:6: "Now we command you, brethren, in the name of our Lord Jesus Christ, that ye *withdraw yourselves from every brother that walketh disorderly,* and not after the tradition [teaching] which he received of us." He continues in verses 14 and 15: "And if any man obey not our word by this epistle, *note that man,* and *have no company with him,* that he may be ashamed. Yet count him not as an enemy, but admonish him as a brother."

Certainly it is evident that in order to vindicate a holy God and to preserve His work from difilement, as well as to rebuke sin and seek the deliverance of brethren who are caught in sin, we are commanded to refuse fellowship with certain of our brethren. However painful and difficult this is, it is Biblical. The Lord give us grace to apply this principle to our current lives and problems with love and patience, and with faithfulness and loyalty to God.

Opportunities for fellowship.

1. Baptist churches throughout history have sought the blessings that flow from a voluntary fellowship with sister churches. These groups of churches came to be called associations. The objective is not a centralizing of power nor of finances. No extensive organization is established. Fellowship and mutual help in missionary activity and other common tasks are purely voluntary. The association must not violate the sovereign independence of the local churches.

This very type of fellowship is indicated among the churches of Macedonia and Achaia (2 Cor. 8; 9) as they joined willingly (8:10, 11) in giving to the needy saints at Jerusalem (Rom. 15:25, 26). There is evidence of some united action beyond the gifts, for one man was "chosen of the churches" to go with the apostle to administer the gifts (2 Cor. 8:18, 19). Here the churches joined their gifts for a common purpose and entrusted them to the care of a representative chosen by them mutually; but there was no "united budget" or coercion.

A bond of fellowship is also indicated among "the seven churches which are in Asia" in Revelation 1, as the Lord walked in the midst of the "seven candlesticks" and addressed to them the seven letters in the second and third chapters. This is further substantiated by the well-known fact that the Epistle to the Ephesians is actually a circular letter which was also sent to other churches of the area. Thus the comradeship and cooperation of those early churches is imitated by the voluntary associations of our Baptist churches today. We have scriptural basis for our associations.

The convention system of this era was unknown to the early church and to the Word of God. The development of the modern system which has overridden the scriptural independence of the local churches is unjustified.

There are definite benefits to our associational fellowships. There is a real danger to a local church in isolationism. A church by itself may either become proud with a feeling that it alone is true to the Lord (as Elijah of old), or it may swing to the opposite extreme in discouragement because the task is too great and there are none to help. It is both humbling and encouraging to fellowship with our sister churches and find in them faithful, fruitful works for the Lord.

Furthermore, these fellowships, or associations, are a means of strength to accomplish some things which cannot be done separately. This is especially true in our missionary work. Smaller churches share in tasks which they could not undertake alone.

"Free-lance" churches, like "free-lance" Christians, suffer a tragic loss in blessings which they should impart to others, as well as in blessings which they should receive.

The common reply from churches who have no associational connections is, "We suffered so much when we joined the Convention that we are not going to join anything else, now that we are free." But actually this reply is not valid, as a Baptist church cannot Biblically join any other group. No association worthy of our fellowship will allow a church to "join." When churches seek one another's fellowship, they come together voluntarily; and they may leave voluntarily. This is the position that true Baptists have always held.

The associational relationship of churches is sufficiently important that we here submit a lengthy quotation on this subject from a volume that has been regarded as a dependable text on Baptist polity and principles for nearly a century. Note particularly the emphasis on the local church and its autonomy. Bible-believing Baptists have rejected all centralization of ecclesiastical authority because the Scriptures reject it. *The New Directory for Baptist Churches* by Edward T. Hiscox, first published in 1894, gives nine pertinent facts concerning associations (pp. 332-337):

> 1. The term *Association* is used in *two* distinct and quite dissimilar senses; by not observing which fact much confusion, and at times no small difficulty, arises in the minds of people.
> *First,* the organized body which meets annually for the transaction of business, is called the *Association.* This body corporate consists of *pastors* and *messengers,* as its constituent elements and active *members.* It has its constitution,

by-laws, its order of business, meets and adjourns, publishes its proceedings, enrolling the names of its pastors and messengers, who alone have the rights of membership in its sessions.

Second, in a somewhat vague and ideal sense all the associated churches, and the geographical limits over which they are scattered, are called the *Association.* Thus we speak of the dearth or the prosperity which prevails in this or that Association, or we say that revivals have, or have not been extensive in such or such an Association. No reference is here had to the organic body which meets annually for business, but to the territorial field, and the local churches, from which the pastors and messengers come.

2. An Association—the organized body that meets for business—is *not* composed of churches, but of individuals, the pastors and messengers. It is a common way of speaking, but a very loose and misleading way, to say it is composed of churches. This arises from a misapprehension, and perpetuates a misunderstanding. A Baptist Church cannot be a member of any other body whatever. It would violate its sacred charter, and lose its identity as the body of Christ, to attempt such a union. And if many churches should enter into organic relations, and constitute an ecclesiastical confederation, the local churches would be absorbed, losing largely their individuality and their independence. Also, in that case, the confederate body would possess legislative and judicial control over the separate congregations. This is the actual *status* of most Christian denominations. But our polity and our traditions repudiate both the inference and the hypothesis on which it rests.

3. But it may be asked, How is it, if churches are not *members* of the body, that the Associations uniformly receive new churches to their number, or dismiss or drop churches from it? The reply is this: Churches are not received to *membership,* though such expressions are often, and indeed ordinarily used; but they are received to *fellowship* and *cooperation;* which fact is evinced, by their pastors and messengers being admitted to *membership,* thus composing its constituent elements.

4. An association is not a *representative* body, in the ordinary acceptation of that term. A Baptist Church cannot appoint persons with delegated authority to act for it, so as to bind it by their action. It cannot transfer its authority and responsibility to any person, or persons whatever. It can appoint persons as committees to perform service for it, and report their doings. If it be still insisted, for the sake of terms, that the churches do meet in the Association, by their representatives, the pastors and messengers, the reply must be—such is not the case, and cannot be, either actually or constructively for a Baptist Church cannot be *represented* by delegates authorized to act for it in any other organization whatever.

5. An Association is a *voluntary* society formed and maintained for mutual help among the churches associated, and for the religious welfare of the field it occupies. It is of human, not of divine authority; it grows out of the sympathies of Christian fellowship, and the need of mutual help. No Church is under obligation to affiliate with it; and any connected Church can withdraw cooperation, at any time, for any reasons which seem to itself sufficient, without prejudice to either its evangelical or its denominational reputation and standing. But while it continues associated, it must abide by the rules and regulations, mutually agreed upon, by which the body is governed.

6. Because an Association is not a representative body, and because a Church cannot be represented in any other organization, and because a Church cannot, even if it would, alienate, or transfer its powers and responsibilities to any man, or body of men, *therefore* an Association cannot legislate for the churches, exercise any authority over them, or bind them in any way by its own action. Whatever is done while in session, is of authority only to those who do it; that is, the members— pastors and delegates. They may make suggestions to the churches, or present appeals, and lay requests before them; to all of which the churches will give such attention as may seem to them right and proper.

7. The fact that the messengers are appointed by their respective churches argues nothing as to their being invested with delegated power. This appointment is made at the request of the Association, and according to its constitutional provisions, as the most convenient and equitable method of constituting the body, not because the appointment carries any ecclesiastical authority with it. These messengers bear the letters and salutations of their churches, and consult with the other members as to the objects for the interest of which they meet.

8. An Association is an *independent* body, not subject to the authority or control of the churches any more than the churches are subject to its authority and control. It frames its own constitution, makes its own by-laws, elects its own officers, and manages its own business, without dictation from anyone. Within its own sphere of action it is just as independent as a Church is within its sphere of action. It fixes the terms of membership and the conditions on which the churches may associate; designates the number of messengers to be sent from each Church, orders its own exercises, meets and adjourns at its own pleasure. If any Church does not approve the proceedings it can refuse to affiliate, and withdraw at any time from the Association, if it thinks best.

9. In the exercise of its independence, also, the Association can refuse to receive its messengers, and drop from its fellowship any Church that has violated the constitution and the original compact, or that has, in any matter deemed vital, departed from the faith and practice of the associated

churches and the denomination. Provisions for such emergencies are made in the constitutions of all Associations; also, the process of fraternal labor to be pursued with the recusant Church before final excision shall be decreed is likewise prescribed.

2. Other areas of fellowship between churches of "like faith and order" are found by cooperation in evangelistic campaigns, missionary conferences, ordination councils, youth camps, magazines that promote a common interest and prayer burden for each other, publication of Sunday school literature, the placing of chaplains in the armed services, and many similar activities. None of these need detract from, but rather should add to, the total effectiveness of each individual testimony.

We do not live unto ourselves (Rom. 14:7). Fellowship is not only a privilege, but a responsibility. We are to bear one another's burdens (Gal. 6:2). ". . . The whole body fitly joined together and compacted by that which every joint supplieth, according to the effectual working in the measure of every part, maketh increase of the body unto the edifying of itself in love" (Eph. 4:16). Through these bonds by which we are united in Christ we should be an unmeasured blessing to each other! "Behold, how good and how pleasant it is for brethren to dwell together in unity!" (Ps. 133:1).

16

Church Councils

CHURCH COUNCILS have long been common among Baptists. However, they are not a New Testament institution. A local church has a sovereign right to ask counsel of sister churches, and the propriety of a council is based upon that right. The meeting in Acts 15 was not a council of churches, but a meeting of the church in Jerusalem (v. 22), convened to determine the answer to questions raised by some of the younger churches.

Councils have no jurisdiction over a local church. As the name indicates, they are advisory only. They have no ecclesiastical authority. They are temporary. They are convened at the invitation of a local church and cease to exist when they adjourn.

Councils may be called for various purposes. The most common are ordination councils and recognition councils. Councils are also called to advise a local church on problems that the church has failed to resolve by itself.

If these internal problems, prompting the calling of a council, involve differences between groups or individuals within the church, and both or all sides of the controversy agree to the council, it is called a mutual council. If only one party to the problem sanctions the call, the council is known as ex parte. An ex parte council is usually fruitless, since only one side of the problem is presented, and a fair and sound judgment is difficult, if not impossible.

A council is normally called by vote of the church but may be called by a group of churches, an individual or a group of individuals. The call is extended to surrounding churches of like faith and order. It is very unwise to invite a non-Baptist church, or a Convention church to give counsel to a separated Baptist church! In all fairness, this should include all sister churches in the area, and not a selected few. Unbiased counsel is to be sought, and "packing" the council is unethical. Usually the invitation asks each church to send its pastor and two messengers.

The invitations should be sent by the church well in advance, preferably at least one month. They should indicate the specific date and hour, place of meeting, purpose of the council, names of the churches and any individuals invited, and who has authorized the council to be called. In a mutual council, if other individuals are included with the church messengers, each party involved in the problem should be permitted to select an equal number of members. Those invited to the council should write the church, indicating whether or not they will be in attendance.

The parties calling the council are not to be members of it, but may attend and present to the group all the information they possess.

Councils are neither legislative nor judicial. They assemble to hear evidence and give counsel, but they are not courts to render verdicts. A local church which calls a council normally accepts the advice given, but is under no obligation to do so. It is still an autonomous church. This principle must be carefully guarded.

Ordination Councils

An ordination council is called by the church of which the candidate is a member. The church has no jurisdiction in ordaining anyone who is not a member. Frequently the pastor and deacons have first examined the candidate in sufficient detail to be assured that they are willing to recommend ordination. Ordination committees in an association (a common practice in conventions) are not a valid Biblical procedure. The local church is sovereign in exercising the right to call a council. It is unwise to call a council to examine a man whom the church is not happy to ordain. Sometimes such action has been taken in an effort to avoid the embarrassment of the church refusing to ordain. This is unfair to the council to expect it to advise against ordination, and thus "save face" for the church. This is also unfair to the candidate, for the refusal of the council to advise ordination is much more public and humiliating to the man than the more private action of the deacons or church. Furthermore, a council may take favorable action on a man who is unqualified rather than be responsible for embarrassing both the candidate and the church. This is tragic and ought never to be done.

No arbitrary educational standards are generally accepted among Bible-believing Baptists, although thorough training is considered very desirable. Ordination is not advisable until a man has a specific call to a church or other door of ministry, and has completed his present course of formal education.

Ordination councils are vital. Churches should make every effort to send their pastors and messengers; and pastors should make all possible sacrifices to attend. The councils should take their responsibilities seriously and question candidates carefully and then seek to reach honest, objective conclusions. Ordaining men who are unsound doctrinally, or otherwise unqualified to serve as ministers, will probably hurt many churches and persons later, and bring dishonor to the Lord.

Ordination by the church does not impart to the man any divine authority or power. It is the recognition by the church of the fact that it believes that God has called and ordained the man as His servant. The ordination by the church constitutes a commendation of the man for public leadership and ministry (see Acts 13:2, 3).

Ordination is not necessarily perpetual. It is valid only as long as the man adheres to the doctrine and conduct which were the basis for his ordination. If he becomes unsound in doctrine, moral conduct or other areas, the church of which he is then a member may, and should, rescind the ordination, regardless of who granted it. Only the church of which a person is a member can exercise discipline. Therefore, a church should not drop a person from membership upon the request of that person if discipline should be exercised. The church has no jurisdiction after the membership has been terminated.[1]

While the ordination council is often held in the afternoon and the ordination service the same evening, it is much to be preferred that the ordination follow at a later date. This gives a council a greater sense of freedom to advise delay of ordination for further study by the candidate if this is needed. The practice sometimes employed of a council recommending ordination, but asking the candidate to do extensive reading on points of doctrinal weakness, is usually dangerous and fruitless. It is better to advise such study, delay a recommendation, and propose that the church call another council in three to six months or a year, depending on the situation.

Adequate time should be allowed the council for thorough examination—perhaps three hours, from 2 P.M. to 5 P.M. In such a case, the church often serves an evening meal for the council, whether or not there is an evening service.

The examination of the candidate is usually divided into three

---

1. It would be in order for the ordaining church, if it has all the facts, to rescind its action to ordain the erring pastor—not as a matter of discipline but to clear its records.

areas: his statement of his conversion to Christ and questioning on this; his statement on his call to the ministry and his preparation, followed by a time of questioning; and his statement of doctrinal convictions, followed by extensive questioning. Usually these questions are asked by anyone on the council. In some areas, the practice is to appoint an examiner who asks most of the questions. The questioning is sometimes reserved until the completion of the candidate's statement and sometimes follows his statement on each doctrine. The method used is commonly decided by vote of the council before the doctrinal statement is given.

It is the practice in some places to require the candidate to read a long paper on his doctrinal position—in some cases as much as an hour or an hour and a half. More commonly a shorter statement is read and more time is allowed for questions. This seems profitable, for the council can in this way more readily determine how conversant the man is with Biblical doctrine and the Scriptures that declare it. Anyone can compile a sound, written statement, especially if help is obtained from others, but the oral response is more indicative of a man's true abilities.

Questioning should be thorough, but should not involve trick questions to embarrass and confuse. The object of the council is to determine the qualifications of the candidate. The moderator should kindly but firmly suppress discussion that aims to promote argument within the council, or display the pet doctrinal hobbies of some individuals.

It is the church that does the ordaining, not the council, although the ordained men on the council are usually invited to assist in the ordination service, whether it is held the same day or at a later date. The council's work is advisory, but serves also to create a wider sphere of confidence and fellowship for a new minister. Conceivably the church could proceed with the ordination even if the council recommended against it. However, this would be most unusual and probably unwise.

The church should have on hand a suitable ordination certificate, properly lettered with the candidate's name. The document can thus be completed and signed with a minimum of delay.

Members of the church should be encouraged to attend the council meeting. It will be very instructive and interesting for them.

Order of service for an ordination council

1. Hymn, Scripture and prayer—moderator from local church.
2. Election of temporary moderator; he then takes the chair.
3. Election of temporary clerk.

4. Reading of church minutes calling the council—church clerk.

5. Roll call of those invited—church clerk.

6. Motion to seat messengers invited and present, or those who arrive later.

7. Motion to formally convene the council.

8. Election of permanent officers (temporary officers or others may be chosen).

9. Motion relative to seating visitors. (The council has no power to enlarge itself without approval by the church, but men of sound doctrinal and ecclesiastical convictions may be invited to sit in the council without vote.)

10. Introduction of the candidate.

11. Instruction of candidate as to procedure, including when questions will be asked, either following entire statement or after each doctrine.

12. Candidate's statement on conversion and questions.

13. Candidate's statement on call to the ministry and preparation, followed by questions.

14. Candidate's doctrinal statement and questions.

15. Motion to terminate examination, and then to excuse the candidate and members of his immediate family and meet in executive session. (If there are many guests or church members, the council may withdraw to another area, rather than dismissing those who are not on the council.)

16. Motion as to recommendation to local church.

17. Recall and notification of candidate.

18. Motion authorizing the clerk to prepare the ordination certificate.

19. Motion making moderator and clerk available to local church in planning ordination service if their help is desired.

20. Motion authorizing clerk to send news items to suitable publications, and to supply the local church and the candidate with a copy of the council minutes.

21. Announcements by church concerning meal, ordination service, etc.

22. Motion to adjourn and dissolve the council.

Order of service for ordination service

1. Suitable music as desired.

2. Reading of council recommendation to the church.

3. Action of church on recommendation.

    4. Scripture reading.

    5. Prayer.

    6. Ordination sermon. (Frequently the candidate has chosen well in advance the man for this message.)

    7. Special music.

    8. Charge to the church.

    9. Offering (often given to the newly ordained man for the purchase of books for his library).

    10. Charge to the candidate.

    11. Laying on of hands and ordination prayer.

    12. The hand of fellowship, by a representative fellow minister.

    13. Presentation of ordination certificate.

    14. Hymn.

    15. Benediction by newly ordained minister.

The order of service varies widely. In some areas the ordination and charges precede the ordination sermon, making it possible to close the service with a message from the Word.

Recognition Councils

During recent decades some Baptist churches have neglected calling recognition councils. This is unfortunate, for it has resulted in problems that could have been avoided.

The historic and customary procedure when a new Baptist church is formed is for that church to call a council of sister churches, including pastors and messengers, to meet together and examine the articles of faith, the constitution, the covenant, the practices of the church and the purposes for organizing. Special care should be exercised by the council to determine whether or not the present practices of the church conform to the standards in the official documents. They may have unimmersed members, may disregard requirements for officers or may be preaching other doctrines. If the council finds that all documents and practices are in keeping with Baptist faith and polity, and the purposes for the organization are justifiable, it then votes to recognize the church as a Baptist church.

As is the case in all Baptist councils, the finding of the council is not binding upon the local church. If the council should decline to recognize the church, it would still have the right to call itself a Baptist church. On the other hand, every other Baptist church in the council would have the right to refuse to accept it into associational fellowship.

The main purpose back of this historic procedure among Baptists is the safeguarding of the general fellowship against the possibility of unwittingly receiving into fellowship churches which are irregular in doctrine or practice. Obviously such care needs to be exercised. It is a very easy matter for a group of people to get together and organize what they call a Baptist church, and then apply for fellowship in an association, offering no other evidence that they are a Baptist church. It is also very easy for an uninformed group of sincere believers to be mistaken and to create a church which is not a Baptist church in its doctrine or polity. If no council is called to examine the documents, usually the errors are not discovered until sometime later, when the association finds that the church in question should never have been accepted into the fellowship because it is not a Baptist church.

A recognition council is a blessing to the church and those who participate. It also constitutes an opportunity for a good testimony in the area concerning the position held by the church and why it is different from the churches in the ecumenical movement.

A recognition council is conducted in much the same manner as an ordination council; the same principles apply.

Order of service for recognition councils

1-9. Same as in ordination council. At this point the council determines procedure, which is usually similar to listing below.

10. Read church covenant. Discussion and suggestions are received. Questions may be answered by the pastor, one of the deacons or other members of the church.

11. Read doctrinal statement and church constitution. Discussion, questions and suggestions. Specific suggestions approved by the council in any of these areas should be recorded and a list of these suggestions given to the church and attached to the minutes of the council. A distinction should be made between recommendations that are made to improve and those that are required in order to approve the church. If basic changes are required, approval should be conditioned upon the action of the church in making the changes. If the problems are serious or extensive, it may be necessary for the church to call another council at a later date.

12. Motion for council to withdraw into executive session.

13. Motion concerning the recommendations and the approval by the council.

14. Reconvene with members of the church to inform of action taken.

15. Receive from church any desired announcements.
16. Authorize clerk to send news of council action to suitable publications.
17. Authorize moderator and clerk to assist church in planning public service if desired.
18. Motion to adjourn and dissolve council.

17

Distinctive Doctrines
of Baptists

LET US MAKE IT clear that there is no truth to the sarcastic charges often heard that Baptists think they are the only people who are going to be in Heaven. No informed Baptist believes or ever said such a thing. Men are saved through faith in Christ, regardless of denominational affiliation.

Nor do we believe any doctrine simply because it is held by Baptists. We believe these things which are precious to us because we believe the Bible and are convinced they are taught therein!

As we speak very candidly about Baptists and their distinctive doctrines, we are in no sense proud or haughty. If we do know the truths of God's Word, it is by His gracious revelation; and we should therefore be humble and grateful to Him.

We also need to be clear on another point. We are well aware that denominations other than Baptists believe *some* of the basic doctrines that are precious to us. Some of these truths are common to one group and some to another. However, for all practical purposes it is correct to state that *none but Baptists* have held *all* of these Biblical doctrines (teachings) down through the years. For instance, Bible-believing Methodists accept the accuracy of the Bible but reject the immersion of believers, the independency of the local church and the sovereignty of God in man's salvation. On the other hand, Presbyterians historically have accepted the accuracy of the Bible and the sovereignty of God, but reject immersion and the independency of the local church. There are other differences, of course, but these illustrate our statement. Baptist believe *all* these things are Biblical. The distinctive doctrinal position which we hold, therefore, is found in the *sum* of these teachings more fully than in each individual doctrine.

Finally, let us clarify a last point: We shall be using the word *Baptist* rather frequently because of the nature of this chapter. We make no apology for doing so, but we wish to make some observations. When we speak of the Baptist denomination, we are not speaking of the Baptist convention. The two are not synonymous. The title *Baptist* names, or denominates, a people who have been marked by certain Biblical doctrines and positions long before there was a convention. People do not become Baptists by joining a convention, nor cease to be such if they leave it.

We do not use this title in a sectarian or divisive sense, but to identify a company of people who hold historically to a blessed Biblical position. We recognize that some who call themselves Baptists have denied these truths and in fact, therefore, are not Baptists. But this happens to any name that may be considered; and every group is called by some name, and as such is a denomination as we here use the word. This is as true of independents, interdenominationalists and Brethren as it is of Baptists. We deny that there is anything carnal in the use of such a title as Baptist, or that there is any superior spirituality involved in avoiding the name. We use it to designate a company of people who, through the years, have been marked by definite doctrinal convictions which we believe are Biblical.

A clear, identifying label is valuable and honest, that people may know the content of a bottle or an organization. Such a label is required by the food and drug laws of our nation. Surely we ought to be equally fair to people by identifying ourselves as Baptists. This is a name that is historically and Biblically significant. It is my conviction that the critical attitude sometimes manifested toward the title *Baptist* frequently results from an unwillingness to accept the full, firm, doctrinal stand represented by the title. Where this is true, we can do nothing to relieve the opposition. The Lord help us, however, not to give any needless offense or any appearance of antagonism toward other brethren in Christ, even if we are separated from them organizationally by our doctrinal convictions.

The Accuracy and the Authority of the Bible

The doctrine of the inspiration of the Scripture is common to all groups within the historic Christian faith; without this, groups cease to be truly Christian. However, among Baptists this doctrine is given an emphasis and an application that are unique.

Our position.   We believe in the verbal, plenary inspiration of the original manuscripts of the Old and New Testaments. The entire Bible is a revelation from God, infallible and entirely free from error of any kind. It is the final authority in all matters of doctrine and of conduct.

Our terms.   By "verbal inspiration" we mean that the Holy Spirit so guided and controlled the men whom He used to write the Scriptures that not only the ideas but the very words they wrote are given to us from God. While He used the style and vocabulary of each man in such a way that it was not a mechanical dictation, He so directed the choice of the words that they are His words and for that reason are pure and perfect words.

By "plenary inspiration" we mean that the entire Bible is fully and equally inspired and that we have a complete revelation from God to man. The Bible does not *contain* the Word of God; it *is* the Word of God. One part is not more accurate than another. No additional revelations are necessary, either in writings or visions. This is the Word of God!

While the doctrine of inspiration applies to the original documents and we do not possess them, this fact provides no basis for uncertainty. Thousands of copies or portions have been found in widely scattered areas, translated into many languages and over a long period of time. These have been diligently compared and provide ample evidence that we possess an accurate text of the original manuscripts. We can therefore read, believe, obey and proclaim our Bible today as the Word of God. I prefer the King James Version for reading, memorizing and preaching, but I find real profit in the comparative study with the American Standard Version of 1901 and other versions. The modern Revised Standard Version, published by the National Council of Churches, reveals the doctrinal bias of the theological liberals who did the translating, and is not to be trusted. Even more serious problems characterize the New English Bible.

The Bible claims to be the Word of God.   We must accept that claim and believe the Book, or, logically, reject the entire Bible as a fraud if we reject its claim to inspiration.

We suggest a few out of many portions to support this teaching: "For the prophecy came not in old time by the will of man: but holy men of God *spake as they were moved by the Holy Ghost*" (2 Pet. 1:21). "All scripture is given by inspiration of God . . ." (2 Tim. 3:16). The Lord Jesus declared, ". . . The scripture cannot be broken" (John 10:35); and, "For verily I say unto you, Till heaven and earth pass, one jot or one tittle shall in no wise pass from the law, till all be fulfilled" (Matt. 5:18). These portions teach verbal, plenary inspiration of the Bible.

The Bible is to be obeyed because it is the Word of God.   This is the reasonable and practical application of the truth which we have been considering. It is of little value to affirm our faith in the doctrine if we refuse to apply the truth to our own lives. We cannot successfully avoid this by spiritualizing the Scripture or by investing the words with new meanings that are more convenient, as do the liberals and the neoorthodox. We dare not sit in judgment upon the Word to make it conform to our standards. The Word must sit in judgment upon us.

We need a proper balance between the study and the practice of Biblical doctrine. Some people talk much about conduct and little about Biblical truth. This leads to fanaticism and carnality, for we must have the Word to direct and to enable Biblical conduct. Apart from the Biblical teaching, our conduct is only the result of human standards which are very faulty. Others talk much about doctrine and little about conduct. This leads to coldness and formality. Ezra sets before us an excellent balance in these things as he prepared his heart to seek the will of the Lord and to do it and to teach it to the people (Ezra 7:10).

A distinctive doctrine.   This doctrine is seen most distinctively among Baptists in this area of practical application of the truth of inspiration. The Bible plainly teaches the immersion of believers; and Baptists have insisted upon obedience even when it involved banishment or death. No argument of expediency or convenience was allowed to overrule the Book. The Bible teaches the independency of the local church; so Baptists historically have refused to establish an organization over the local churches (until the recent encroachments gained by the Convention in our day, and which we have repudiated).

This subjection to the authority of the Word is also revealed in the nature of the services in our churches. The preaching of the Bible is the central feature in our meetings. Therefore, it is not the formal type of service marked by rituals, sacraments and other inventions of men. The music, prayers, testimonies and other parts of the meeting prepare us for, and focus our attention upon, the ministry of God's Word.

Furthermore, the subject matter of the messages reveals this distinctive emphasis. Bible-believing Baptist churches are characterized by a Bible-teaching, gospel-preaching ministry. (Tragically in this day, some who call themselves Baptists are not, for they do not honor His Word.) This is in contrast to the textual sermons and orations so common in many places. The latter actually give expression to the philosophy of the preacher and usually reflect more fully the modern authors he has been reading than they do the Bible, even when the message is generally orthodox. Baptists appeal to the Scripture, not to history, philosophy, science and art for their inspiration and instruction in spiritual things, although we do gladly acknowledge the value of these things in their proper spheres. We are not here charging that no one else teaches the Word of God, but it is very commonly a distinctive mark of Baptist churches.

Dangers to avoid.   We must guard this position zealously. It is the citadel of our doctrinal soundness and of our spiritual power. May we continue to try all things by the Word of God and to hold fast to the things that are good. May we also continue to remember that the Word is the Sword of the Spirit, without which we are impotent.

We must avoid three major points of danger if we are to hold fast the faithful Word, as we are exhorted in Titus 1:9.

1. We must discern and deny the satanic assault upon the accuracy and authority of the Bible. Satan has already robbed the major part of Christendom of all confidence in the Word of God. While this is not our primary danger at the moment, it can happen to us unless we resist him and understand his wiles. There is urgent necessity for us to speak out against this blasphemous attack of the liberals so that we may warn others who are not informed.

2. We must resist our own inclination to laziness. This keeps us from searching the Word for ourselves. We can be grossly misled by well-meaning people, accepting as "gospel truth" things contrary to the Bible, unless we become students of the Word and also accept the doctrine of inspiration.

3. We must refuse resolutely to follow the current trend which exalts the intellect of man at the expense of the authority of the Scripture. God warns: "Beware lest any man spoil you through philosophy and vain deceit, after the tradition of men, after the rudiments of the world, and not after Christ" (Col. 2:8). We certainly should put no premium upon ignorance. We are confident there is no conflict between intelligence and spirituality. But there is a very dangerous movement, even among evangelicals, as efforts are being made to justify the Bible intellectually with the science and philosophy of our day. There is a terrible danger of intellectual pride that causes men to soften toward the rationalism of unbelievers. Our Bible needs no defense and no apology. There is no room for softness. We are at war with a ruthless enemy!

Soul Liberty

Soul liberty is a phrase that has long been common among Baptists. Before discussing it positively, we should note that it is not a doctrine that justifies license or lawlessness. It is not a justifiable basis for the indulgence of self-will. Pressed to this point it becomes totally unbiblical and unbaptistic and contradicts the major doctrine of the authority of the Scripture. As someone else once stated, "This doctrine has two aspects: soul liberty plus soul compulsion."

Soul liberty is the implementation of the truth that we must "obey God rather than men" (Acts 5:29). Every man must give answer to God individually, and therefore no other man, and no church, can act as his conscience now. He has the right to interpret the Scripture for himself and the responsibility to answer to God for the way in which he does so. He has, as a believer, the Holy Spirit to guide and enable him, apart from any other ministry of man or of the church. "The anointing which ye have received of him abideth in you, and ye need not that any man teach you . . ." (1 John 2:27). ". . . Let every man be fully persuaded in his own mind" (Rom. 14:5).

This right to interpret the Word logically necessitates the other liberties of freedom of speech and freedom of worship. Throughout their history, Baptists have contended for these liberties for others as well as for themselves. Our early American history reveals that primarily it was the Baptists who established freedom of relgous worship in our own land. The Puritans had begun religious persecutions here after fleeing such persecutions in Europe.

Baptists believe, therefore, that they have a right to preach the whole counsel of God, including the warnings against false teachings and false teachers. But while they oppose and expose the error, they defend the right of others to hold those errors if they insist. In other words, they contend against error with truth rather than with violence or suppression.

Soul liberty is properly limited by responsibility to Scripture and by the rights and liberties of our fellowmen. Our liberties end where the other man's liberty begins. For example, we have no liberty to put powerful loudspeakers on our churches and disturb the services across the street or to blast our message into the privacy of homes against the will of the homeowners. The law rightfully says we are disturbing the peace.

Furthermore, soul liberty does not justify an individual's continually opposing the doctrines, the practices or the decisions of his church. His brethren also have the right and liberty of their convictions! If his convictions oppose theirs, he should have the right to express himself and to exercise the privilege of trying patiently and lovingly to convince them that he is right. But if he fails in this, he must either subject himself happily to the decision of the group or move to some other church where he can practice his convictions in harmony with those of like faith. His liberty does not give him the right to violate the liberty of others.

It is vital that we practice this truth carefully. Since we have profound convictions concerning Biblical things, it is easy for us to become intolerant of the rights of others. We dare not compromise the truth as we know it, "for whatsoever is not of faith is sin" (Rom. 14:23). But we must respect the rights of our brethren to practice the same liberty, remembering that every man stands or falls to his own master (Rom. 14:4).

The Sovereignty of God

We discuss this subject briefly as a summary of a major doctrine of most Baptists, as distinct from that of many groups.

Baptists believe that God, as an intelligent, rational Being, has a plan for man and for the universe and that He has the authority and the will to operate that plan. Many other groups place a great deal of emphasis upon the free will of man as though God had left the outcome of His plans to the fickle decisions of men who are sold under sin and dead in sin.

We believe that God seeks the sinner, rather than the sinner seeking God (Gen. 3:9; Rom. 3:11). It is God Who provides salvation in His infinite grace; it is God Who implements that salvation in individual men whom He has chosen in Christ before the foundation of the world (Eph. 1:4). We believe that those who trust in Christ are eternally secure in Him, for we are kept by the power of God (1 Pet. 1:5; Phil. 1:6; Heb. 7:25; John 10:27-30).

The king's heart is directed by the Lord (Prov. 21:1). If God is God, then He is sovereign in wisdom, power and grace! Some people are strangely afraid of this truth, as though they felt that we would protect ourselves against unfair treatment from Him by insisting that His will be limited by our wills. This seems to be nothing less than the sin of unbelief! "Shall not the Judge of all the earth do right?" (Gen. 18:25).

This confidence in Him does not produce fatalism, as is sometimes charged, for the outcome of His plan is not the result of blind chance. It is fulfilled by our infinitely wise God, "who worketh all things after the counsel of his own will" (Eph. 1:11). Neither does this truth remove missionary vision and a burden for souls, as some say. No group of people in all Christendom has a greater missionary vision than Baptists who hold this truth. The same Lord Who ordains men to eternal life (Acts 13:48), ordains men in His service (John 15:16). He Who calls men to Himself through Jesus Christ (John 6:44; 2 Cor. 5:19) has sent us to preach Christ to them (2 Cor. 5:20; Rom. 10:12-15).

Praise God that we can commit our way to the Lord, trust also in Him, and He will bring it to pass (Ps. 37:5)!

We are not contending for some mystical sanctity in the Baptist name, but we are contending earnestly for that blessed body of truth which Baptists have believed through the ages. We are happy to be identified with that host of Bible-believing men and women through the past centuries who stood for this truth both in life and in death. A review of the history of those centuries, to recall the bitter opposition heaped upon our Baptist forefathers by both Protestants and Romanists, will help us to appreciate the significance of this name which has been given to us. (That title was given to us by the enemies of the truth in that day.) May we be as loyal and uncompromising to that truth as were those dear saints who have gone before us.

We live in a day of compromise, a day when many of those who affirm belief in the great doctrines of the faith are pleading for compromise and softness in our convictions. May the Lord help us to hold the truth in love and to be steadfast and unmovable. The truth which we believe and proclaim is not our own; it is a revelation from God.

Several of these doctrines have received consideration in greater detail in previous chapters. They are included here in brief outline form to help unify the thinking on the distinctive doctrinal position of Baptists. Occasionally we hear such remarks as: "Why all this talk about doctrine? I think we ought to study the Bible." This, of course, is unwarranted, for "doctrine" simply means "teaching," and doctrinal study is a specific effort to determine the teachings of the Bible. This must be accomplished by comparing one Scripture with another to discover the total message of the Word upon each subject. It cannot be done successfully by studying only one brief portion, for in this way we are in danger of reaching false conclusions from which other portions of the Bible would guard us.

We are warned against "teaching for doctrines the commandments of men" (Matt. 15:9). This was the trouble with the leaders in Christ's day who had developed their own teachings which were not true to His Word. Christ warned the people to beware of their "leaven." "Then understood they how that he bade them not beware of the leaven of bread, but of the doctrine of the Pharisees and of the Sadducees" (Matt. 16:12). It is a danger against which we must guard by searching the Scripture daily to see if these things be so (Acts 17:11).

The Scripture is clear on the positive side. Paul writes about "sound doctrine," "good doctrine," "my doctrine" and "the doctrine of God our Saviour'' (1 Tim. 1:10; 4:6; 2 Tim. 3:10; Titus 2:10). He exhorts us to ''give attendance . . . to doctrine,'' ''exhort with . . . doctrine,'' ''in doctrine shewing uncorruptness'' and to ''adorn the doctrine . . .'' (1 Tim. 4:13; 2 Tim. 4:2; Titus 2:7, 10).

It is evident, therefore, that we are responsible to believe and to proclaim the doctrines of the Word of God. We are also responsible to discern between the true and the false doctrines and to reject and repudiate the false.

The apostle Paul was repudiating the false doctrine of the resurrection taught by Hymenaeus and Philetus in 2 Timothy 2:17 and 18. In 2 Peter 2 and 3, Peter was revealing the errors of false doctrines about the Lord and about His coming. John is similarly engaged in his epistles. This type of ministry, teaching true doctrine and repudiating the false, therefore, occupies a surprisingly large portion of the Scriptures. Baptists who have been marked by such a ministry are following a Biblical example.

As we consider the following doctrines, it is well to remind ourselves that some other groups of Christians hold some of these doctrines. However, few, if any, hold all of them. We believe that all these teachings are Biblical and that we must hold them if we are to maintain faithful, New Testament churches.

A Pure, Regenerate, Baptized Church Membership

A church is a spiritual, not a social, economic or political organization. It is charged by the Lord to preach the Word and to worship the Lord. This is impossible for men who have not been born again. There is no Biblical warrant for taking children into the church until we have their definite assurance that they have been born again. Confirmation at the age of twelve is no substitute for regeneration! Neither is there any justification for taking adults into the church with the hope that in these surroundings they will be saved. The Scripture is clear: ''Then they that gladly received his word were baptized. . . . And the Lord added to the church daily such as should be saved [such as were being saved]'' (Acts 2:41, 47). ''Ye also, as *lively* stones, are built up a spiritual house, an holy priesthoood, to offer up spiritual sacrifices, acceptable to God by Jesus Christ'' (1 Pet. 2:5; Rom. 1:7; 1 Cor. 1:2; 2 Cor. 1:1 and Eph. 1:1).

Baptism was practiced by the apostles, promptly and uniformly, with all who confessed Christ. It was definitely the door to discipleship. It is interesting to note in the record of Philip and the eunuch (Acts 8) that Philip had so instructed the eunuch about baptism while preaching the gospel to him, that his first move in confessing faith in Christ was a request to be baptized (vv. 35, 36).

Baptists believe the Word teaches that men should be saved and immersed to belong to the church. (See chapter 2.) They also believe that it teaches they are to be pure and godly and maintain good works. The church is His, and we are not to dishonor Him with worldliness and other sin. (See Titus 2:11-15.)

Faithful obedience to this truth is vital if there is to be power in the church through an ungrieved Holy Spirit. It is vital also if sound doctrine and practice are to be maintained in the days ahead. Nothing will more rapidly corrupt the doctrine and ministry of a church than an unregenerate group within it. They do not have the spiritual discernment to divide between truth and error. Neither do they have a spiritual hunger after truth nor a burden to proclaim a pure, Biblical message. Human reason soon displaces divine revelation, and expediency displaces the commandments of God.

Sovereign, Indpenedent Local Churches

We live in a day of centralized power and authority. This has been increasingly true, both in church and state. The historic, Biblical, baptistic position on the sovereign independency of local churches is being challenged increasingly. Now there is a drive toward centralization into an ecumenical, one-world church, not merely the denominational overlordship. This doctrine of an independent local church is, therefore, vital and timely. We must resist the pressure to abandon this truth and to follow the popular path.

Voluntary fellowship and cooperation were evidently practiced by the New Testament churches, as indicated in chapter 3. Nothing is given in the Word, however, to justify the organization of any authority over the local church. To do so is to impose a human program upon a divine institution.

Where denominational machines are interposed between the soul and the Lord, there are several dangers: (1) They remove certain responsibilities from the people and eventually weaken the people spiritually by providing a "program" and reducing their conscious responsibility directly to the Lord. "Loyalty to the denomination" is the common watchword rather than loyalty to the Lord and His Word. (2) Centralized power attracts carnal men to the leadership of these organizations. (3) These machines give dangerous power and influence to these carnal men and provide serious snares and temptations to many sincere and earnest men in such leadership. (4) This unscriptural authority eventually results in imposing an utterly unscriptural program upon the local churches.

God never sanctioned any human organizations to impose authority over the churches. When saved men and women meet in one company to pray and preach and to seek God's will, it is difficult for the Devil to corrupt their ministry. When intermediate authorities are established, the need for prayer is less and less apparent and the will of the Lord is more easily confused with the decisions of the men in authority.

Two Officers: Pastors and Deacons

As has been shown, these are the two officers of a local church. The Scripture sanctions no others over them.

We again warn here that this statement is not any reflection upon members within a church who have been given special responsibilities by that church, such as trustees, treasurer, ushers. The church has a sovereign right to do so. However, the pastor and deacons are the spiritual leaders of the church, and no officers are over them in the exercise of that leadership. Men who are worthy of such leadership will not be inflated with pride over such positions, but rather will be humbled with a sense of the need for His direction and blessing. (See chapter 5.)

Two Ordinances: Baptism and the Lord's Supper

We have no right to invent more ordinances, nor to neglect either of these two. These are symbolic acts which portray the two basic facts in our relation to Christ: our union with Him and our communion with Him. (See chapter 7.)

Separation of Church and State

This is another Biblical teaching in which Baptists have led the way in the interpretation of, and obedience to, the Bible.

The state is a divine institution (Rom. 13) given to preserve the rights and liberties of the righteous and to restrain and punish the evil. While it is ideal that civil leaders trust and obey the Lord and seek His wisdom, yet the government encompasses all men, both believers and unbelievers. Hence, God has never given to civil rulers the right to administer the church, which is a spiritual body. As Christians and also citizens of our country, we have a responsibility to exercise our rights in civil government to support righteousness and oppose wickedness. It is certainly unwise for a Christian to become so absorbed in such activities, however, that he forgets his primary ministry is in spiritual things.

The church is also a divine institution, entrusted with the evangelization of sinners, the edification of saints and the exaltation of the Savior. Only saved persons rightfully belong to this company. The officers and members of a church are not authorized in the Word to divide and jeopardize their spiritual ministry by seeking authority over the civil government.

History is a long, sad record of the tragic results of disobedience on both sides. If we value our own liberties and those of our children, if we would be obedient to the Word of God, we shall contend earnestly for the strict observance of this Biblical principle.

Strenuous efforts are being made by some to get government support for parochial (or church) school buses. This is an attack upon a vital principle, and we are opposed to such support for others or for ourselves. The appointment of a representative of our government to the papal state was another attack upon this principle. It is always true that eternal vigilance is the price of liberty. Unless we decry such practices and openly contend for these Biblical convictions, the forces of greed will move in and combine church and state for the advantages of wealth and power. As a matter of fact, this will finally come to pass in the Great Tribulation period, with the result of oppression and violence. (See Revelation 17.)

The Priesthood of All Believers

This is a precious Biblical teaching. It assures the right of each individual believer to worship the Lord without the help of any other person. We are invited as brethren in Christ to "enter into the holiest by the blood of Jesus" (Heb. 10:19). This could not have been done under the Old Testament. At that time, only the high priest could go into the holy of holies as a representative with blood for his own sins and those of his people.

A major part of Christendom today has no concept of this liberty. Men generally feel that the preacher is a priest in a certain sense and has liberties and powers with God that are beyond those of the common man. This is not true. He may use that privilege more faithfully than many, but the way is open for every believer (Heb. 10:19-22).

The teaching in the Word is clear. The words of 1 Peter 2:1-10 reveal that even the babes in Christ are included in the company of those who, trusting in Christ the living Stone, are "an holy priesthood, to offer up spiritual sacrifices, acceptable to God by Jesus Christ" (v. 5). We do not now offer blood sacrifices as the priests of Israel. Christ offered one sacrifice for sins forever and sat down because the redemptive work was completed (Heb. 10:12-14). But we do offer the sacrifice of praise (Heb. 13:15), the sacrifice of our gifts (Heb. 13:16—the word *communicate* refers to material giving) and the sacrifice of ourselves (Rom. 12:1). It is our privilege and duty to intercede before God for one another, as the priests of old went before God in behalf of the people. The command to pray "always with *all* prayer . . . with *all* perseverance . . . for *all* saints" is addressed to *all* brethren (Eph. 6:10-18).

The priests of the Old Testament were consecrated to God (Lev. 8) and wore special clothing befitting their office (Exod. 39:27-29). The privileges which we have as priests require also proper consecration and proper "clothing." Now it is not a matter of material clothing, but we must be clothed in the garments of salvation and the robe of righteousness (Isa. 61:10). The priestly garments were of linen (Exod. 39:27-29), which is typical of the righteous acts of the saints (Rev. 19:8).

The blood of the ram of consecration was placed upon the right ear, the thumb of the right hand and the great toe of the right foot of Aaron and his sons (Lev. 8:22-24). It was thus declared that the ears were consecrated to hear the voice of God, the hands to do the service of God and the feet to walk in the paths of God. Now, the One Who has made us kings and priests has "washed us from our sins in his own blood" (Rev. 1:5, 6). It is now our "reasonable service" (Rom. 12:1) to consecrate our ears, our hands, our feet—yes, to present our bodies a living sacrifice—so we may indeed be a holy priesthood.

As priests, we are not only to be consecrated to holiness by the blood, but we are to be characterized by holiness in our conduct. Perhaps these holy requirements impose a price which many are unwilling to pay, and they shun the responsibilities of the priesthood. The easy way is to look upon the preacher as the responsible party! It is his job to be holy; it is his job to pray and offer sacrifices! But this is not God's way.

18

Creeds of the Church

THROUGHOUT THE CENTURIES churches have sought to formulate their concepts of Biblical doctrines in articles of faith or creeds. The oldest such statement of which we know dates back at least to the early part of the fourth century and is called the Apostles' Creed. It is accepted generally in Christendom, including Roman, Greek and Protestant churches. It is characterized by great brevity, containing only 110 words:

> I believe in God the Father Almighty, maker of heaven and earth:
> And in Jesus Christ, His only Son, our Lord,
> Who was conceived by the Holy Ghost,
> Born of the Virgin Mary,.
> Suffered under Pontius Pilate,
> Was crucified, dead and buried.
> He descended into hades:
> The third day He rose again from the dead.
> He ascended into heaven, and sitteth on the right hand of God the Father Almighty;
> From thence He shall come to judge the quick and the dead.
> I believe in the Holy Ghost; the holy catholic church; the communion of saints; the forgiveness of sins; the resurrection of the body; and the life everlasting. Amen.

As doctrinal error increased, creeds became more detailed. The Nicene Creed, adopted in A.D. 325, follows generally the Apostles' Creed, but it sets forth more clearly and strongly the fundamental truth of the deity of Christ. Many other creeds appeared through the centuries, many of which mingled error with truth, as the leaders and movements forsook Biblical doctrine and followed the doctrines of men. A brief but helpful discussion of this subject is found in the widely used volume *The New Directory for Baptist Churches* by Edward T. Hiscox.

Some Baptist groups in this century (such as the American Baptist Convention) have refused to subscribe to any doctrinal statement. They have said that creeds are not baptistic and that the Bible is a sufficient statement of faith. (In view of the wide doctrinal divergence within the American Baptist Convention, one rightfully suspects that their antipathy toward a statement of faith stems from a refusal to commit themselves to a specific doctrinal position.)

History certainly does not support the claim that officially accepted creeds or confessions are foreign to Baptists. The English Baptists issued one confession in London in 1644 and an enlarged London Confession in 1689. With some changes, this was adopted in 1742 by the Philadelphia Association and has been known as the Philadelphia Confession. The text of this confession, which is unusually long, has been published in *The Hiscox Guide for Baptist Churches*. (We do not recommend the general emphasis of this volume. It has been greatly altered from the original text by Dr. Hiscox. Among other errors, it now repudiates the Biblical position of the independence and autonomy of the local church and supports the Convention's position on ecumenism.)

The New Hampshire Confession was published in 1833. The text of this confession is available in *The New Directory for Baptist Churches* by Dr. Hiscox. It constitutes basically the articles of faith of the General Association of Regular Baptist Churches and of some other Baptist associations. It has been revised in some measure, particularly by adding a premillennial position to the article on eschatology. Copies of this revision are available in pamphlet form from the General Association of Regular Baptist Churches, P. O. Box 95500, Schaumburg, Illinois 60195.

A primary emphasis among Baptists, historically, has been the conviction that the Bible is a divine revelation and is a complete and infallible guide and standard of authority in matters of faith and conduct. We base our faith upon the Word of God and not upon creeds or confessions. We defend what we believe by the Word of God.

Some may ask, in view of the above facts, what is wrong with the claim of the Convention that the Bible is a sufficient confession of faith and that they need no other. The answer should be obvious. Men have imposed their own interpretations upon the Bible. Presbyterians, Methodists, Adventists, Catholics, Jehovah's Witnesses and a host of others declare that they believe the Bible, yet they all believe conflicting doctrines. Creeds and confessions adopted by different denominations set forth the specific teachings held by these groups. To many, these creeds have become authoritative, and thus have largely displaced the Bible in the thinking of the people.

Baptists have also adopted creeds or confessions. This is right and proper. The term *creed* comes from the Latin word *credo,* which means, "I believe." To Baptists, creeds are not the basis of faith. By such creeds we define, delineate and declare what we believe the Word of God teaches. Thus we eliminate misunderstanding, ambiguity and confusion. We are able to set forth clearly to all who desire to know what we hold to be Biblical truth. But to us, as Baptists, these doctrines are true, not because they are baptistic or because they are contained in a Baptist confession; these truths are in the confession because we are convinced they are what the Bible teaches! This viewpoint is vital and is an emphasis that must never be surrendered.

19

Covenants, Articles of Faith and Articles of Incorporation

BAPTISTS HAVE HISTORICALLY used three official documents: a constitution, a covenant and articles of faith. The first provides for the orderly conduct of the church and its business. The second is a sacred agreement between the members of the church whereby they express their devotion to the Lord and to each other. The third sets forth clearly the doctrinal truth held by the members.

A fourth document is now important legally in our present culture, articles of incorporation. The purpose of this document is to give legal status to the church and certain other advantages that will be discussed later in this chapter.

Prospective members are to read and express their acceptance of the first three of these vital instruments before being received into fellowship. Members are to maintain familiarity with the content of the documents and sincerely seek to fulfill them in daily life.

Church Covenants

Two forms of a church covenant are submitted here. The first is the one in common use in Baptist churches. It was written early in the nineteenth century by Dr. J. Newton Brown. The second is a current revision of the first, updating terms and emphases.

A Church Covenant

Having been led, as we believe, by the Spirit of God to receive the Lord Jesus Christ as our Savior, and on the profession of our faith, having been baptized in the name of the Father and of the Son, and of the Holy Ghost, we do now in the presence of God, angels, and this assembly, most solemnly and joyfully enter into covenant with one another, as one body in Christ.

We engage therefore, by the aid of the Holy Spirit, to walk together in Christian love; to strive for the advancement of this church, in knowledge, holiness, and comfort; to promote its prosperity and spirituality; to sustain its worship, ordinances, discipline, and doctrines; to contribute cheerfully and regularly to the support of the ministry, the expenses of the church, the relief of the poor, and the spread of the gospel through all nations.

We also engage to maintain family and secret devotion; to religiously educate our children; to seek the salvation of our kindred and acquaintances; to walk circumspectly in the world; to be just in our dealings, faithful in our engagements, and exemplary in our deportment; to avoid all tattling, backbiting, and excessive anger; to abstain from the sale and use of intoxicating drinks as a beverage; and to be zealous in our efforts to advance the kingdom of our Savior.

We further engage to watch over one another in brotherly love; to remember each other in prayer; to aid each other in sickness and distress; to cultivate Christian sympathy in feeling and courtesy in speech; to be slow to take offense, but always ready for reconciliation, and mindful of the rules of our Savior, to secure it without delay.

We moreover engage that when we remove from this place, we will as soon as possible unite with some other church, where we can carry out the spirit of this covenant and the principles of God's Word.

A Church Covenant

Having been led by the Holy Spirit to receive the Lord Jesus Christ as our Savior, and on the public confession of our faith, having been immersed in the name of the Father, and of the Son, and of the Holy Spirit, we do now, in the presence of God and this assembly, solemnly and joyfully enter into covenant with one another, as one body in Christ.

We purpose, therefore, by the aid of the Holy Spirit, to walk together in Christian love; to strive for the advancement of this church in knowledge, holiness and comfort; to promote its prosperity and spirituality; to attend its services regularly; to sustain its worship, ordinances, discipline and doctrines; to give it a sacred preeminence over all institutions of human origin; to give faithfully of time and talent in its activities; to contribute cheerfully and regularly, as God has prospered us, to the support of the ministry, the expenses of the church, the relief of the poor, and the spread of the gospel throughout all nations.

We also purpose to maintain family and private devotions; to train our children according to the Word of God; to seek the salvation of our kindred and acquaintances; to walk circumspectly in the world; to be just in our dealings, faithful in our engagements, and exemplary in our conduct; to avoid all gossip, backbiting and unrighteous anger; to abstain from all forms of activity—including the sale and use of intoxicating beverages—which dishonor our Lord Jesus Christ, cause stumbling to a fellow believer or hinder the winning of a soul to Christ; to be zealous in our efforts to advance the cause of Christ, our Savior; and to give Him preeminence in all things.

We further purpose to encourage one another in the blessed hope of our Lord's return; to watch over one another in brotherly love; to remember each other in prayer; to aid each other in sickness and distress; to cultivate Christian sympathy in feeling and courtesy in speech; to be slow to take offense, but always ready for reconciliation, and, mindful of the rules of our Savior, to seek it without delay.

We moreover purpose that when we remove from this place we will as soon as possible unite with some other church of like faith and order where we can carry out the spirit of this covenant and the principles of God's Word. If there is no such church, we shall seek, with the Lord's help, to establish one.[1]

Articles of Faith

Each church needs a clear statement of faith which sets forth great Biblical doctrines which it believes.

The articles of faith are not designed to be the foundation or the defense of our faith. They simply define and declare what we believe the Word of God teaches on these vital doctrines.

The following is provided to assist churches which are preparing or revising their doctrinal statement. It is a current revision and enlargement of a doctrinal statement used by many Baptist churches, the original basis of which was the historic New Hampshire Confession of Faith.

---

1. Copies of this covenant may be purchased from Regular Baptist Press.

1. The Scriptures

We believe in the authority and sufficiency of the Holy Bible, consisting of the sixty-six books of the Old and New Testaments, as originally written; that it was verbally and plenarily inspired and is the product of Spirit-controlled men, and therefore is infallible and inerrant in all matters of which it speaks.

We believe the Bible to be the true center of Christian unity and the supreme standard by which all human conduct, creed and opinions shall be tried (2 Tim. 3:16, 17; 2 Pet. 1:19-21).

2. The True God

We believe there is one and only one living and true God, an infinite Spirit, the Maker and supreme Ruler of Heaven and earth; inexpressibly glorious in holiness, and worthy of all possible honor, confidence and love; that in the unity of the Godhead there are three Persons, the Father, the Son and the Holy Spirit, equal in every divine perfection and executing distinct but harmonious offices in the great work of redemption (Exod. 20:2, 3; 1 Cor. 8:6; Rev. 4:11).

3. The Holy Spirit

We believe that the Holy Spirit is a divine Person, equal with God the Father and God the Son and of the same nature; that He was active in the creation; that in His relation to the unbelieving world He restrains the Evil One until God's purpose is fulfilled; that He convicts of sin, of righteousness and of judgment; that He bears witness to the truth of the gospel in preaching and testimony; that He is the Agent in the new birth; that He seals, endues, guides, teaches, witnesses, sanctifies and helps the believer (John 14:16, 17; Matt. 28:19; Heb. 9:14; John 14:26; Luke 1:35; Gen. 1:1-3; John 16:8-11; Acts 5:30-32; John 3:5, 6; Eph. 1:13, 14; Mark 1:8; John 1:33; Acts 11:16; Luke 24:49; Rom. 8:14, 16, 26, 27).

4. The Devil, or Satan

We believe in the reality and personality of Satan, the Devil; and that he was created by God as an angel but through pride and rebellion became the enemy of his Creator; that he became the unholy god of this age and the ruler of all the powers of darkness and is destined to the judgment of an eternal justice in the lake of fire (Matt. 4:1-11; 2 Cor. 4:4; Rev. 20:10).

5. Creation

We believe the Biblical account of the creation of the physical universe, angels and man; that this account is neither allegory nor myth, but a literal, historical account of the direct, immediate creative acts of God without any evolutionary process; that man was created by a direct work of God and not from previously existing forms of life; and that all men are descended from the historical Adam and Eve, first parents of the entire human race (Gen. 1, 2; Col. 1:16, 17; John 1:3).

6. The Fall of Man

We believe that man was created in innocence (in the image and likeness of God) under the law of his Maker, but by voluntary transgression Adam fell from his sinless and happy state, and all men sinned in him, in consequence of which all men are totally depraved, are partakers of Adam's fallen nature, and are sinners by nature and by conduct, and therefore are under just condemnation without defense or excuse (Gen. 3:1-6; Rom. 3:10-19; 5:12, 19; 1:18, 32).

7. The Virgin Birth

We believe that Jesus was begotten of the Holy Spirit in a miraculous manner, born of Mary, a virgin, as no other man was ever born or can be born of woman, and that He is both the Son of God and God the Son (Gen. 3:15; Isa. 7:14; Matt. 1:18-25; Luke 1:35; John 1:14).

8. Salvation

We believe that the salvation of sinners is divinely initiated and wholly of grace through the mediatorial offices of Jesus Christ, the Son of God, Who, by the appointment of the Father, voluntarily took upon Himself our nature, yet without sin, and honored the divine law by His personal obedience, thus qualifying Himself to be our Savior; that by the shedding of His blood in His death He fully satisfied the just demands of a holy and righteous God regarding sin; that His sacrifice consisted not in setting us an example by His death as a martyr, but was a voluntary substitution of Himself in the sinner's place, the Just dying for the unjust, Christ the Lord bearing our sins in His own body on the tree; that having risen from the dead He is now enthroned in Heaven, and uniting in His wonderful Person the tenderest sympathies with divine perfection, He is in every way qualified to be a suitable, a compassionate and an all-sufficient Savior.

We believe that faith in the Lord Jesus Christ is the only condition of salvation. Repentance is a change of mind and purpose toward God, prompted by the Holy Spirit, and is an integral part of saving faith (Jonah 2:9; Eph. 2:8; Acts 15:11; Rom. 3:24, 25; John 3:16; Matt. 18:11; Phil. 2:7, 8; Heb. 2:14-17; Isa. 53:4-7; 1 John 4:10; 1 Cor. 15:3; 2 Cor. 5:21; 1 Pet. 2:24).

9. Resurrection and Priesthood of Christ

We believe in the bodily resurrection of Christ and in His ascension into Heaven, where He now sits at the right hand of the Father as our High Priest, interceding for us (Matt. 28:6, 7; Luke 24:39; John 20:27; 1 Cor. 15:4; Mark 16:6; Luke 24:2-6, 51; Acts 1:9-11; Rev. 3:21; Heb. 8:6; 12:2; 7:25; 1 Tim. 2:5; 1 John 2:1; Heb. 2:17; 5:9, 10).

10. Grace and the New Birth

We believe that in order to be saved, sinners must be born again; that the new birth is a new creation in Christ Jesus; that it is instantaneous and not a process; that in the new birth the one dead in trespasses and in sins is made a partaker of the divine nature and receives eternal life, the free gift of God; that the new creation is brought about by our sovereign God in a manner above our comprehension, solely by the power of the Holy Spirit in connection with divine truth, so as to secure our voluntary obedience to the gospel; that its proper evidence appears in the holy fruits of repentance, faith and newness of life (John 3:3; 2 Cor. 5:17; 1 John 5:1; Acts 16:30-33; 2 Pet. 1:4; Rom. 6:23; Eph. 2:1, 5; Col. 2:13; John 3:8).

11. Justification

We believe that justification is that judicial act of God whereby He declares the believer righteous upon the basis of the imputed righteousness of Christ; that it is bestowed, not in consideration of any works of righteousness which we have done, but solely through faith in the Redeemer's shed blood (Rom. 3:24; 4:5; 5:1, 9; Gal. 2:16; Phil. 3:9).

12. Sanctification

We believe that sanctification is the divine setting apart of the believer unto God, accomplished in a threefold manner; first, an eternal act of God, based upon redemption in Christ, establishing the believer in a position of holiness at the moment he trusts the Savior; second, a continuing process in the saint as the Holy Spirit applies the Word of God to the life; third, the final accomplishment of this process at the Lord's return (Heb. 10:10-14; 3:1; John 17:17; 2 Cor. 3:18; 1 Cor. 1:30; Eph. 5:25-27; 1 Thess. 4:3, 4; 5:23, 24; 1 John 3:2; Jude 24, 25; Rev. 22:11).

13. The Security of the Saints

We believe that all who are truly born again are kept by God the Father for Jesus Christ (Phil. 1:6; John 10:28, 29; Rom. 8:35-39; Jude 1).

14. The Church

We believe that a local church is an organized congregation of immersed believers, associated by covenant of faith and fellowship of the gospel; observing the ordinances of Christ; governed by His laws; and exercising the gifts, rights and privileges invested in them by His Word; that its officers are pastors and deacons, whose qualifications, claims and duties are clearly defined in the Scriptures. We believe the true mission of the church is the faithful witnessing of Christ to all men as we have opportunity. We hold that the local church has the absolute right of self-government, free from the interference of any hierarchy of individuals or organizations; and that the one and only Superintendent is Christ through the Holy Spirit; that it is scriptural for true churches to cooperate with each other in contending for the faith and for the furtherance of the gospel; that each local church is the sole judge of the measure and method of its cooperation; that on all matters of membership, of polity, of government, of discipline, of benevolence, the will of the local church is final (1 Cor. 11:2; Acts 20:17-28; 1 Tim. 3:1-13; Acts 2:41, 42).

We believe in the unity of all New Testament believers in the Church which is the Body of Christ (1 Cor. 12:12, 13; Eph. 1:22, 23; 3:1-6; 4:11; 5:23; Col. 1:18; Acts 15:13-18).

15. Baptism and the Lord's Supper

We believe that Christian baptism is the single immersion of a believer in water to show forth in a solemn and beautiful emblem our identification with the crucified, buried and risen Savior, through Whom we died to sin and rose to a new life; that baptism is to be performed under the authority of the local church; and that it is prerequisite to the privileges of church membership.

We believe that the Lord's Supper is the commemoration of His death until He come, and should be preceded always by solemn self-examination. We believe that the Biblical order of the ordinances is baptism first and then the Lord's Supper, and that participants in the Lord's Supper should be immersed believers (Acts 8:36, 38, 39; John 3:23; Rom. 6:3-5; Matt. 3:16; Col. 2:12; 1 Cor. 11:23-28; Matt. 28:18-20; Acts 2:41, 42).

16. Separation

We believe in obedience to the Biblical commands to separate ourselves unto God from worldliness and ecclesiastical apostasy (2 Cor. 6:14—7:1; 1 Thess. 1:9, 10; 1 Tim. 6:3-5; Rom. 16:17; 2 John 9-11).

17. Civil Government

We believe that civil government is of divine appointment for the interests and good order of human society; that magistrates are to be prayed for, conscientiously honored, and obeyed, except in those things opposed to the will of our Lord Jesus Christ, Who is the only Lord of the conscience, and the coming King of kings (Rom. 13:1-7; 2 Sam. 23:3; Exod. 18:21, 22; Acts 23:5; Matt. 22:21; Acts 5:29; 4:19, 20; Dan. 3:17, 18).

18. Israel

We believe in the sovereign selection of Israel as God's eternal covenant people, that she is now dispersed because of her disobedience and rejection of Christ, and that she will be regathered in the Holy Land and, after the completion of the Church, will be saved as a nation at the second advent of Christ (Gen. 13:14-17; Rom. 11:1-32; Ezek. 37).

19. Rapture and Subsequent Events

We believe in the premillennial return of Christ, an event which can occur at any moment, and that at that moment the dead in Christ shall be raised in glorified bodies, and the living in Christ shall be given glorified bodies without tasting death, and all shall be caught up to meet the Lord in the air before the seven years of the Tribulation (1 Thess. 4:13-18; 1 Cor. 15:42-44, 51-54; Phil. 3:20, 21; Rev. 3:10).

We believe that the Tribulation, which follows the Rapture of the Church, will be culminated by the revelation of Christ in power and great glory to sit upon the throne of David and to establish the millennial kingdom (Dan. 9:25-27; Matt. 24:29-31; Luke 1:30-33; Isa. 9:6, 7; 11:1-9; Acts 29:29, 30; Rev. 20:1-4, 6).

20. The Righteous and the Wicked

We believe that there is a radical and essential difference between the righteous and the wicked; that only those who are justified by faith in our Lord Jesus Christ and sanctified by the Spirit of our God are truly righteous in His esteem; while all such as continue in impenitence and unbelief are in His sight wicked and under the curse; and this distinction holds among men both in and after death, in the everlasting felicity of the saved and the everlasting conscious suffering of the lost in the lake of fire (Mal. 3:18; Gen. 18:23; Rom. 6:17, 18; 1 John 5:19; Rom. 7:6; 6:23; Prov. 14:32; Luke 16:25; Matt. 25:34-41; John 8:21; Rev. 20:14, 15).

Articles of Incorporation

Incorporation is a legal action which, in a sense, gives the organization the status of an individual before the law. It is not necessary to incorporate in order to establish a Biblical church. Many churches have never taken this step. However, there are dangers imposed needlessly upon a church by failure to incorporate, and certain limitations are also imposed.

Each church should be incorporated for the following reasons:

1. To designate and hold exclusively a name for the church, thereby distinguishing it from all others. Conditions may develop which will make this very important.

2. To enable the church to purchase, lease or sell property as a church. Apart from incorporation, the title must (in most states) be held in the names of some individual members.

3. To hold insurance and protect individual members against responsibility and personal loss in such matters as liability suits against the church.

4. To enable the church to make contracts, hold mortgages and incur liabilities.

5. To qualify the church to receive tax deductible donations.

State laws vary, and it is wise for a church to consult a lawyer, or at least to secure a copy of the state law from the secretary of state, in accordance with the laws of that state. A certificate of incorporation will then be issued to the church and filed in the county courthouse. Many states require the filing of an annual report and the payment of a small fee.

If a church is uncertain about whether or not it is incorporated properly, the records at the county courthouse will supply the answer.

We submit a suggested form of articles of incorporation for the assistance of the church seeking this information. Certain changes may be necessary in some states; for instance, some states require a registered agent for the corporation. The chairman of the deacons or trustees would be the logical party for this position.

Articles of Incorporation
of the
_____ Baptist Church of _____, _____.

We, the undersigned, desiring to become incorporated under the provisions of the laws of _____, as a religious, non-profit corporation, do hereby make, execute and adopt the following articles of association, to wit:

First, the name assumed by this corporation, and by which it shall be known in law, is _____ Baptist Church of _____, _____.

Second, the location of said church shall be in the (township, city or village) of _____, county of _____, and state of _____, post office address _____

Third, the time for which this corporation shall be created shall be perpetual.

Fourth, the members of said church shall worship and labor together according to the teachings of the New Testament, as set forth in the articles of faith adopted by this church.

Fifth, this church shall have the authority to conduct a Baptist church in accordance with the Word of God, the articles of faith, the covenant and the constitution of this church. It shall have the right to own, buy or sell tangible properties, both real and personal, in its own name and through properly elected officers, when authorized by vote of the church.

This church shall be independent and autonomous, not subject to any ecclesiastical control whatsoever from any convention, conference, association, council, group or individual outside of the local church; but it shall have the right to voluntarily affiliate with any association or council of Bible-believing churches separated from the apostasy, and the right to disassociate from any group with which it may have become affiliated.

The government of this church shall be vested in its membership. Voting privileges shall be extended to members in good and regular standing fourteen years of age and over, except that the minimum age shall be twenty-one years for the transaction of all legal matters.

Sixth, no profit shall ever accrue to the benefit of any individuals from the assets, holdings or other transactions in which this corporation may become involved.

In the event of the dissolution of this corporation, all of its debts shall be fully satisfied. None of its assets or holdings shall be divided among the members, or other individuals, but shall be irrevocably designated by corporate vote, prior to dissolution, to such other nonprofit religious corporations as are in agreement with the letter and spirit of the articles of faith adopted by this church, and in conformity with the requirements of the United States Internal Revenue Service Code of 1954 (Section 501 C-3).

In witness whereof, we, the parties hereby associating for the purpose of giving legal effect to these articles, hereby sign our names and places of residence:

Done at the (township, city or village) of _____, county of _____, and state of _____, this _____ day of _____, 19_____.

(Signatures)   (Residence)

_____   _____
_____   _____
_____   _____

State of _____
County of _____, S. S.
   I, _____, a Notary Public, do hereby certify that on the _____ day of _____, 19_____,

_____

(Names of Incorporators)

personally appeared before me and in my presence signed the foregoing document in the respective capacities therein set forth and declared that the statements therein contained are true.

IN WITNESS WHEREOF, I have hereunto set my hand and seal the day and year above written.

(SEAL)   (Notary Public)

20

A Church Constitution

THE SCRIPTURES lay down broad principles concerning the church. It is clear that the officers are to be pastors and deacons with specific qualifications, and that they are chosen by the church. The method of their selection is left to the church, and needs to be settled by each church to avoid confusion. The local church meets to transact its business, as illustrated in the disciplining of wayward members (Matt. 18:17; 1 Cor. 5). The Scripture does not, however, give details as to how to determine who is qualified to vote in such a meeting. Clarity on this point is essential to internal harmony. What is the name of the church? How many deacons are to be elected? When is the annual meeting to be held? Who is qualified to serve as teachers? These and many similar details are not spelled out in the New Testament, but may be settled by consent of the members of a local church, in harmony with the principles of the Word of God. Such practical regulations are logically stated and preserved in an orderly manner in a constitution.

The Lord is a God of order, not of confusion, as evidenced in both creation and revelation. He has commanded us to do everything decently and in order (1 Cor. 14:40). A constitution, if drawn up wisely and prayerfully, is a major step toward order and decency in the conduct of a church. It should provide Biblical, ethical and orderly methods of business procedure. If these items are determined clearly in advance of the time when they may become problems, the solution can be calm and objective, and much friction and strife can be avoided.

Many churches have ignored their constitutions through the years; thus no one knows where a copy can be found, or if one ever existed. Other churches have constitutions that have not been revised in many decades and do not meet the problems current in our generation. Some church constitutions were drawn up by leaders who did not hold baptistic, New Testament doctrine and practices.

Churches in any of the above situations will show real wisdom to appoint a committee to recommend any needed revisions, or to draw up a constitution if none is available. (The pastor ought to be a member of that committee.) Such recommendations must be brought to the church for prayerful consideration and decision before they can be incorporated into the constitution or a constitution be approved.

It will be wise for the committee to secure copies of constitutions from other sound Baptist churches. Help may also be secured from the department of practical theology in one of our sound Baptist schools.

It may be well to consult a lawyer on some of the legal aspects to avoid serious future problems. For instance, in New York State trustees in a Baptist church must number three, six, nine or twelve, and they must be elected in a corporate business meeting in which only members twenty-one years of age or older are allowed to vote. Furthermore, unless the church specifically provides that none can vote except active members of the church, the state law allows nonmembers who attend or who support the church to vote in the corporate meeting. Every constitution should protect the rights of the church members on this point. State laws vary, and each church is under obligation to conduct its business in a legal manner (Rom. 13).

The temptation in drawing up a new constitution or in revamping an old one is to consider the people involved rather than the Biblical principles. This is unsound and foolish. We must adhere to the Word of God even if we offend people who are not subject to it. For example, some churches have failed to require immersion for membership simply because one or more friends might not join the church because of this Biblical standard. Failure at this point allows the number of unimmersed members to multiply. Eventually there is a major division and many members are lost. What is still more serious, the church has compromised the truth, having feared the face of men more than the face of God.

Baptists are convinced that the Word of God is the final authority in all matters of faith and conduct. This basic principle is not altered by the acceptance of a doctrinal statement and a constitution. These instruments are only the mutually agreed upon expression of the Biblical principles in a simple, condensed and accessible form.

We suggest the following constitution as a pattern to churches writing a constitution or remodeling an old one. Naturally, changes will need to be made to adapt to local situations. Some of these have been indicated by italics, such as the number of deacons, the size of a quorum, etc. These will vary with the size of the church, the convictions of the members and other factors.

Constitution
of the
_____ **Baptist Church of** _____, _____
Adopted _____ 19_____
(date)

The Preamble

Reposing our faith wholly in the Lord Jesus Christ for our salvation, and believing in the teachings of the Holy Bible as the plenarily and verbally inspired Word of the living God, we have affiliated ourselves with one another as a body of immersed believers, and we adopt this constitution as a declaration of our convictions so that we may carry on the Lord's work decently and in order.

Article I—Name

The name of this organization shall be _____ Baptist Church, _____, _____. It is incorporated as a nonprofit corporation under the laws of the state of _____.

Article II—Purpose

Our purpose is to glorify God by conducting a Baptist church in accordance with the Word of God, the articles of faith, the covenant and the constitution of this local church, promoting the worship of our God, edifying believers, teaching the whole counsel of God, administering the ordinances and Biblical discipline, seeking to win the lost to Christ through personal witnessing and the preaching of the gospel, carrying on a vigorous missionary program around the world, establishing other Baptist churches, defending the faith, and maintaining a good testimony for Christ in our community by godliness and good works.

Article III—Associations

Section 1

This church shall be an independent, autonomous church, subject only to Jesus Christ, the Head of the Church. It has the right to cooperate and associate with other Biblical groups on a voluntary basis. There shall be no cooperation with any group that permits the presence of apostates or apostasy, or that endorses groups that permit the presence of apostates or apostasy.

Section 2

This church shall fellowship with the General Association of Regular Baptist Churches as long as the Association is characterized by Biblical convictions and vigorous opposition to apostasy and compromise. If the GARBC forsakes its present Biblical position, this church shall take appropriate action to withdraw from its fellowship.[1]

Article IV—Articles of Faith
(Insert your articles of faith.)[2]

Article V—Membership

Section 1–Reception of Members

A. This church shall be composed of members who profess to be saved by grace, through faith, and who have been baptized following their confession of faith in Christ, by single immersion in the name of the Father, the Son and the Holy Spirit.

B. All persons desiring to unite with this church shall meet with the pastor and deacons, and shall give testimony of conversion and Christian experience, and affirm acceptance of and adherence to the articles of faith, constitution and covenant of this church.

C. Upon the recommendation of the pastor and deacons, candidates shall be presented to the church. A *three-fourths* vote of members present and voting is required to approve an individual for membership.

D. Members may be received in one of four ways:
   (1) By baptism following salvation.
   (2) By letter from a church of like faith and order.
   (3) By confession of faith (when impossible to secure a church letter), having been saved and immersed.
   (4) By restoration.

Section 2–Discipline of Members

A. It is vital to the testimony of this church and the glory of our Lord that the purity of the church be preserved and its peace protected. With these ends in view, it shall be the duty of the pastor and deacons to seek diligently to reclaim any member known to be living in disregard of his Biblical

1. The state association may also be included here.

2. See suggested articles of faith in chapter 19.

and covenant obligations. It is specifically directed that the pastor and deacons move with promptness and vigor in dealing with anyone who is obstructing the work or disturbing the peace of the church by slander, falsehood, gossip, conspiracy or other unfair and unchristian methods. It is recognized that a Baptist church must be a democracy in which the majority shall rule. It is recognized further that while the minority has the right of private opinion in all questions and the right of appeal in any constitutional and proper manner, it shall not have the right to engage in secret or open propaganda, or of deliberately disturbing the peace and interrupting the work of the church. It is further recognized that when the church, by regular order and proper vote, has determined upon a course of action, that course becomes the duty of every member of the church. If any member cannot conscientiously follow the decision of the church, he is to quietly and peacefully withdraw from the membership.

B. If a member is walking disorderly in conflict with the above principles, or is involved in any known immorality, dishonesty or public scandal, and such member cannot be restored to fellowship through confession and correction of his sins, he shall be dealt with on the basis of Matthew 18 and 1 Corinthians 5. His case shall be brought before the church by recommendation of pastor and deacons. (See H.) He shall be given a statement of the charges against him, and he shall have opportunity to present his case before the church. The church may vote to remove him from the membership if the charges and evidence warrant such action. In less serious matters, such a person may be placed under discipline and on the inactive membership list by vote of the church. He shall be restored to active membership only by vote of the church after satisfactory evidence is given of scriptural repentance and confession.

C. During the last quarter of each year the pastor and deacons shall review the membership roll. Any member habitually absent from the services of the church without due cause, and who is negligent to spiritual duties, shall be removed from active membership by vote of the church, upon recommendation of the pastor and deacons, and placed on the inactive membership list. The individual shall be informed of this action. This section shall be implemented only after faithful efforts to reclaim the member. Restoration to active membership shall be by vote of the church, upon recommendation of the pastor and deacons, only after there is satisfactory evidence of a renewed spiritual walk.

D. No person on the inactive membership list shall be entitled to vote, hold office or teach.

E. Pastor, deacons and members shall make a sincere effort to reclaim spiritually those on the inactive list. During the last quarter of each year the pastor and deacons shall review the inactive members. After one year of inactive status they shall be recommended to the church to be dropped from the membership. A permanent card file of these former members shall be maintained for continued, prayerful effort to reclaim them for Christ and the church.

F. In the event of differences between members, it is recommended that they be settled personally in accordance with Matthew 18:15 and 16.

G. If a member desires to prefer charges against another member, including violation of covenant obligations or of immoral, improper or unchristian conduct, such charges must be submitted to the pastor and deacons in writing, and must be duly signed by the accuser.

H. In order to prevent unnecessary public scandal, the pastor and deacons may hear the charges, pro and con, in any disciplinary case, if this is mutually satisfactory with the accused and the accuser. If dismissal is recommended by pastor and deacons, the recommendation must be presented to the church, preferably without details, for final action. The entire matter must be brought before the church at the request of the accused, or of the church. No member may be dismissed except by vote of the church.

I. No nonmember shall be permitted in such a church meeting (as witness, defense or otherwise) without permission of *three-fourths* of the members present and voting.

Section 3–Dismissal of Members

A. Dismissal shall be by death, letter or exclusion.

B. Any member in good standing may be granted a letter of transfer to any church of like faith and order upon its request. The letter shall be sent to the church with which the member wishes to unite.

C. A letter of dismissal without recommendation may be sent to any other church.

D. No member who has conducted himself in such a manner as to be cited for disciplinary action may be dropped from membership at his own request since such a procedure would remove him from the authority of the church.

Section 4–Additional Regulations

A. The church shall vote on each candidate before baptism, to receive him into membership following baptism.

B. This church shall not practice the public dedication of babies.

C. Only active members shall be entitled to vote or hold office.

D. Only active members shall serve as regular teachers in the church, Sunday school or other groups.

E. The church shall conduct regularly, or periodically, according to need, classes for new members. These shall be taught by the pastor or some other competent leader. They shall include instruction on such things as the ordinances, church government, responsibilities of church members, stewardship, prayer, Bible reading, witnessing for Christ, the General Association of Regular Baptist Churches and basic doctrines (including separation to God from worldliness and apostasy).

F. It shall be deemed proper to receive members or grant letters at any meeting of the church. If disciplinary action is involved, it shall require a special business meeting of the church, the purpose of which shall be announced by letter to the members of voting age at least two weeks in advance.

Article VI—Ordinances

Section 1–Baptism

Those professing faith in Christ shall, upon authorization of the church, be immersed in water by the pastor or someone else appointed by the church. Only those shall be baptized who are being received into the church membership. Immersion, as a believer, shall be a prerequisite to church membership.

Section 2–The Lord's Supper

The Lord's Supper shall normally be served to the assembled church by the pastor, or some other person authorized by the church, on the first Sunday morning of each month, or at such other time as may be decided by pastor and deacons, or by the church. Since it is the Lord's Table, none that are His shall be barred, but the pastor shall frequently state the scriptural order, which places baptism as a prerequisite to the Lord's Supper, and shall explain the meaning of the ordinances. The elements shall be unleavened bread and grape juice. The Lord's Supper shall not be served outside of a church meeting.

Article VII—Officers and Boards

Section 1–Officers of the Church

    A. The elected officers of the church shall be pastor (or pastors), deacons, trustees, clerk, financial secretary, treasurer and Bible school superintendent.

    B. No one shall be elected to office who has not been a member of this church for at least one year; except that upon recommendation of pastor and deacons a person may be considered by the church for office after six months of membership.[3]

    C. All officers shall be spiritually mature, of unquestioned Christian character, loyal to the Word of God, dedicated and devoted to the Lord Jesus Christ and to the spiritual and material welfare of this church. They shall also be faithful in attendance and participation, both in regular services and business meetings of the church. Their moral conduct shall be beyond reproach and free of carnal indulgences, such as the use of intoxicating beverages, tobacco in all forms, narcotic drugs and other worldly practices. In the light of 1 Timothy 3, the home and family relationships must be considered, as well as individual qualifications.

    D. All officers shall normally assume their duties on January 1. Retiring officers shall hold office until the terms of newly elected officers begin.

    E. Any officer unable or unwilling to fulfill the duties of his office shall resign. If any officer refuses to subscribe to the articles of faith, the constitution and the church covenant, his resignation shall be requested by the deacons. If it is not received within a reasonable time, the office shall be declared vacant by vote of the church.

---

3. This regulation manifestly cannot apply to a new church.

Section 2–The Pastor

A. A candidate for the pastorate shall be carefully examined by the pulpit committee as to his salvation, doctrine, Christian conduct and call to the ministry. If he has served in other churches, his ministry there should be explored. He shall be required to state his acceptance of and adherence to the articles of faith, constitution and covenant of the church. Any differences which he holds concerning these documents should be submitted to the pulpit committee in writing. He shall also state in writing any differences which he holds relating to groups and associations with which this church is in fellowship. The pulpit committee shall present only one man at a time for the consideration and vote of the church.

B. A call to a pastor shall be extended at a meeting of the church called for that purpose and announced from the pulpit for two Sundays immediately preceding the date of the meeting. A *three-fourths* majority of those present and voting shall be necessary for a call. Voting shall be by ballot. A written call and agreement shall be presented to the prospective pastor, giving details of church-pastoral relationship, including salary, housing and car allowances, insurance, vacations, etc., after these matters have been discussed with the pastor and approved mutually.

C. The pastor shall continue in office until he resigns or is dismissed by a *two-thirds* majority of those present and voting at a special meeting called for that purpose. Such a meeting shall be announced from the pulpit for two Sundays immediately preceding the date of such a meeting. (See Article IX, Section 2, F.)

D. The pastor shall give the church not less than thirty days nor more than sixty days notice of his intention to discontinue as pastor. The church shall give the pastor not less than sixty days notice of dismissal. If, in the judgment of the church, the conduct of the pastor justifies immediate termination of his ministry, the church may declare the pulpit vacant and pay two months salary beyond that date.

E. The pastor shall have charge of the spiritual welfare of the church; he shall preach the gospel, teach the Word and have charge of the services of the church; he shall administer the ordinances and perform the usual duties of a Baptist minister.

F. The pastor shall moderate the business sessions of the church. In his absence, the chairman of the deacons shall call the meeting to order and the church shall elect a moderator. If the pastor is to be under discussion in a business session, another moderator shall be elected, and the pastor and his family shall withdraw from the meeting.

G. The pastor shall be an ex officio member of all boards and committees. He shall also be a member of this church.

H. Other workers, such as Christian education director, youth or music director, may be called by the church, but are to be individuals fully approved by the pastor and shall work under his direction.

Section 3–Deacons

A. The board of deacons shall consist of *nine* men elected by the church. Three shall be elected each year for a term of three years.

B. It shall be the duty of the deacons to assist the pastor in promoting the spiritual welfare of the church; to be his helpers and counselors; to exercise prudent watchcare over the church membership; to seek out such members as need alms; to visit the sick; to examine with the pastor candidates for church membership; to assist at baptisms, their wives assisting the ladies; and to supervise the preparation and distribution of the Lord's Supper.

C. They shall appoint a chairman and secretary from their number, keep minutes of their monthly meetings in a permanent record, and report quarterly and annually to the church.

D. They shall constitute the pulpit committee, recommending candidates for the pastorate.

E. They shall appoint ushers to serve at all meetings of the church.

F. They shall administer the deacons' fund.

G. The deacons shall serve as trustees of this church, representing this corporation as its agent. They shall not have authority to sell, lease, give away or dispose of church property in any manner to exceed *$250* in value; nor to mortgage or encumber the same with debt to exceed the above amount, except as the church shall order the same by a corporate act. They shall be responsible for the care and upkeep of the physical properties of the church, including the hiring and supervision of a custodian. All projects involving the expenditure of more than *$250* are to be submitted to the church for approval except in routine matters. They shall approve bills before payment is made by the treasurer.[4]

Section 4–Clerk
A. The church clerk shall have charge of the official correspondence and shall keep a record of all business meetings of the church and the advisory board, entering the minutes of the meetings of the two groups in separate books. The clerk shall keep in a bound book a record of the membership, of baptisms and of the reception and dismissal of members. The clerk shall perform such other duties as properly belong to the office, making quarterly and annual reports to the church.
B. The clerk shall provide the financial secretary and the treasurer promptly with a transcript of the minutes of each church business meeting in which authority is granted for the disbursement or transfer of funds.
C. The clerk shall certify annually to the bank the names of officers who are authorized to have access to the safety deposit boxes and to sign checks for disbursement of funds.
D. Upon his retirement or removal from office, he shall deliver to his successor, or the chairman of the board of deacons, all records, files, and/or other papers belonging to the church, and shall present the same with all contents complete to the date of surrender of such documents.

Section 5–Financial Secretary
A. It shall be the duty of the financial secretary, together with one or more of the deacons, to count and record in a permanent record all monies received in the offerings of the church. This shall be done following each service of the church.

4. If a trustee board is desired, distinct from the deacons, delete G in section 3, decrease number of deacons and add:
Section 4–Trustees
A. The board of trustees shall consist of *six* men, elected by the church, in accordance with the corporate laws of this state. Two shall be elected each year for a term of three years.
B. Define duties as in Section 3, C and G.

    B. Records shall be kept in accordance with written instructions issued by the auditing committee and approved by the advisory board.

    C. The financial secretary shall be responsible for depositing all funds in the bank, including monies received from organizations within the church or from individuals.

    D. The financial secretary shall provide the treasurer with a record of all monies received and deposited, specifying the distribution into various funds, as indicated by the donors or by special offerings.

    E. The chairman of the deacons shall assume the duties of the financial secretary in the absence of the latter, except that he may not assume the duties of the treasurer as outlined in Section 6 simultaneously.

Section 6–Treasurer

    A. The treasurer shall be responsible for the recording of all financial transactions in permanent records and shall make quarterly and annual reports to the church.

    B. The treasurer shall pay the bills of the church after they have been approved by the trustees. He shall write, sign, record and mail all checks. Checks shall be countersigned by a person authorized by the advisory board, other than the financial secretary. The chairman of the deacons shall assume the responsibility of signing checks in the treasurer's absence, except that he shall not perform the duties of the financial secretary as outlined in Section 5 simultaneously.

    C. The treasurer shall keep the books of record and report the financial transactions in accordance with written instructions issued by the auditing committee and approved by the advisory board.

Section 7–Bible School Superintendent

    A. The superintendent shall have general supervision over the Sunday Bible school, teachers and officers. He shall carry out the program established by the Christian education committee and shall report quarterly and annually to the church.

    B. The Christian education committee shall appoint all teachers and officers for the Bible school, in consultation with the pastor.

Section 8–Advisory Board

A. The advisory board shall consist of all officers of the church as named in Article VII, Section 1, A.

B. It shall meet at the call of the pastor, or in the absence of a pastor, the chairman of the deacons. The pastor shall be the moderator; the chairman of the deacons shall be the vice-moderator.

C. The clerk shall keep the minutes and include a report on the activities of this board in his regular reports to the church.

D. It shall be the duty of this board to prayerfully consider major matters of church business or of policy and to recommend to the church for action such matters as are deemed worthy.

E. It shall be the duty of this board to determine the literature to be used in the educational program of the church. The Christian education committee shall make recommendations concerning the literature.

Article VIII—Committees

Section 1–Budget Committee

A. The budget committee shall consist of two deacons (appointed by the deacons), two trustees (appointed by the trustees),[5] the financial secretary, the treasurer and one other member of the church to be designated by the advisory board.

B. The duties of the committee shall be to prepare the budget for the ensuing year for presentation to the church for its approval at the annual meeting.

C. The committee shall function throughout the year to recommend budget revisions to the church as may be deemed necessary.

Section 2–Nominating Committee

A. This committee shall be composed of at least five members. During October, the advisory board shall select one person from each of the following groups to serve on the committee: deacons, trustees,[6] Bible school, missionary organization and two from the church at large.

5. If elected separately from deacons.

6. If elected separately from deacons.

B. The committee shall submit a list of nominees for all offices to be filled. This list shall be posted in the church building at least one Sunday prior to the election. When qualified candidates are available, two or more shall be nominated for each office.

C. Before posting the nominations, the committee shall approach each nominee and secure consent to serve in harmony with the pastor and the constitution of the church, if elected.

D. They shall provide ballot forms for the annual election.

E. Members who wish to submit nominations should give their suggestions in writing to the nominating committee at least three weeks before the election to enable the committee to ascertain qualifications under this Section and Article VII, Section 1, B and C. No nominations shall be made from the floor.

Section 3–Auditing Committee

A. This committee shall consist of two members appointed by the advisory board following the annual election.

B. It shall audit all accounts of the church and its organizations and certify same, reporting at the annual business meeting.

C. The auditing committee, subject to the approval of the advisory board, shall be responsible for establishing the procedures and methods to be followed by the financial secretary and treasurer in maintaining the financial records.

D. The church may vote to authorize the audit by a professional auditing firm rather than by a committee.

Section 4–Christian Education Committee

A. The Christian education committee shall consist of the pastor, the director of Christian education,[7] one deacon, one trustee,[8] the Bible school superintendent, an advisor from the Bible training fellowships and two other members of the church. They shall be appointed by the advisory board following the annual meeting. The chairman shall be other than the Bible school superintendent.

B. This committee shall supervise and coordinate the general

7. If there is such.
8. If elected separately from deacons.

teaching programs of the church in the Bible school, Bible
training fellowships, vacation Bible school and other special teaching programs, and shall make recommendations
to the advisory board concerning the literature to be used.
The advisory board shall make final decisions on the literature.

C. It shall constitute a committee for appointing all teachers
and officers as applicable to the various teaching sections
of the church, and shall assign rooms to the various
groups.

Section 5–Missionary Committee

A. This committee shall consist of the pastor, the chairman of
the deacons, chairman of trustees,[9] president of the missionary organization, the Bible school superintendent and
three other members of the church appointed by the advisory board.

B. It shall recommend the missionary projects to be supported by the church and the auxiliary organizations. Suggestions from such organizations may be submitted to the
committee for consideration and recommendation.

C. It shall draft an annual missionary budget to be submitted
to the budget committee for its action at least three weeks
before the annual meeting of the church.

D. It shall maintain contacts with missionaries supported by
the church, and encourage prayer for, and church-wide
interest in, these and other missionaries.

Section 6–Hospitality Chairman

This chairman shall be appointed by the advisory board, and
shall be responsible to arrange hospitality for visiting speakers, in
consultation with the pastor.

Section 7–Additional Committees

A. A music committee, a flower committee, an advertising
committee and others deemed necessary may be appointed by the advisory board.

B. If a building committee is needed, it shall be nominated by
the advisory board and elected by the church.

C. All committees shall report quarterly and annually to the
church unless otherwise instructed.

---

9. If there is such.

Article IX—Meetings

Section 1–Public Worship

A. Public worship services shall be held regularly, morning and evening, on the Lord's Day. These services shall not normally be given over to anything but prayer and the preaching and teaching of the Word, with an appropriate musical ministry. Any other special presentation shall be subject to approval by the pastor and deacons. Neither shall they be merged into union services with other denominations.

B. At least once each week there shall be a meeting for prayer and praise.

C. It shall be the practice of this church to observe the Lord's Supper at least once a month, at which time it may be appropriate that the covenant be read.

Section 2–Business Meetings

A. The official church year shall begin January 1 and close December 31.

B. The annual meeting shall be held following the prayer meeting on the second Wednesday after the first Sunday in January.

C. The quarterly meeting shall be held following the prayer meeting on the second Wednesday of each of the following months: April, July and October. At this time, written reports shall be read as required by the constitution.

D. The annual election of officers shall be held following the prayer meeting on the second Wednesday in December.

E. The day for business meetings may be changed at the discretion of the church.

F. Special business meetings may be called at any time, providing public notice be given of the same on the Sunday preceding; except as otherwise stipulated in this constitution, or required by state law. (See Article V, Section 4, F, and Article VII, Section 2, C.) Routine business such as receiving members or granting letters may be transacted when necessary at any stated meeting of the church without regard to the above requirements. Special meetings may be called by the pastor, the board of deacons or any *ten* unrelated families who are members of the church and request such of the clerk, providing the particular object, or objects, of the meeting are clearly stated in the notice, and no other business shall be transacted in such a meeting.[10]

G. Only members *fourteen* years of age and above shall be eligible to vote. Only members twenty-one years of age and above[11] shall be eligible to vote upon corporate matters such as buying, selling or mortgaging of property, or election of trustees.

H. *Twenty* members shall constitute a quorum.[12]

Section 3–Rules of Order of Business

The ordinary rules of deliberative assemblies shall be observed in the transaction of business, as set forth in *Parliamentary Law*, F. M. Gregg, or *Robert's Rules of Order Revised*, Henry M. Roberts.

Section 4–Order of Business Meetings

A suggested order of business follows:

1. Reading and approval of minutes of previous meetings
2. Clerk's report
3. Treasurer's report
4. Deacons' report
5. Trustees' report
6. Bible school superintendent's report
7. Advisory board's report
8. Reports from other standing committees
9. Reports from special committees
10. Reports from departments of the church
11. Election of officers[13]
12. Unfinished business
13. New business
14. Adjournment

10. In some states, such as Ohio, it may be advisable to require in the constitution that written notice be mailed to each member at least one week in advance.

11. Or whatever age is required by state law.

12. A definite number is much to be preferred over a percentage. A percentage quorum necessitates a knowledge of the exact number of active members on the date of each business meeting. Failure to determine these facts and record them in the minutes has resulted in strife and legal entanglements. A *small* quorum is desirable to assure ability to transact business. The church is protected from abuse by requiring adequate announcements of meetings.

13. According to this constitution, this is to be handled in a separate meeting.

Article X—Church Organizations

Section 1–The Sunday Bible School

A. The purpose of the Bible school is to win each pupil to the Lord Jesus Christ as personal Savior, and to instruct him in the Word and in Christian living, including church attendance and membership.

B. All class officers of junior high age and above shall be members of the church.

C. All officers and teachers of the school shall be appointed annually and shall be members of this church in good standing. Anyone whose conduct or teaching is considered injurious to the class, school or church shall, upon recommendation of the superintendent and the Christian education committee, be referred to the deacons for necessary action.

D. All teachers and officers must first be approved by the Christian education committee. Approval of the literature shall be the responsibility of the advisory board.

Section 2–Bible Training Fellowship

A. The purpose of the Bible training fellowship is to train Christian young people and adults for Christian service.

B. All officers of the junior high age and above shall be members of the church.

C. All counselors must first be approved by the Christian education committee. The literature shall be approved by the advisory board.

Section 3–Subsidiary Organizations

A. No subsidiary organization of the church shall engage in any practice or hold any policy contrary to the general position of the church itself. All officers and regular teachers shall be members of the church.

B. All such organizations are self-governing but are subject finally to the control of the church in accordance with its constitution and voted church policies.

Article XI—Missions

It shall be the policy of this church to support only missions engaged principally in evangelization and establishment of Baptist churches (schools, hospitals and similar ministries must be kept subordinate to the primary objectives). They shall be known to be in hearty agreement with our confession of faith, both in doctrine and practice. They shall be Baptist in both name and practice, and normally shall be missions approved by the General Association of Regular Baptist Churches. Christian schools and social agencies, such as homes for the aged, children's homes, etc., shall be considered an appropriate part of the missionary program.

Article XII—General

Section 1–Use of the Church Property and Name
   A. Use of the property for other than regularly scheduled meetings shall first be approved by the trustees.
   B. All gatherings off the church property held in the name of the church shall be subject to the approval of the pastor and deacons.
   C. No secret society will be permitted to hold services in the church. The funeral of any person so associated may be held in the church if conducted by an approved minister. The society may take charge of the remainder of the service after the body leaves the church.
   D. No pastor or pulpit orator will be permitted to preach in the church who fails to confess clearly the fundamentals of the faith once delivered unto the saints (Jude 3). Any visiting speaker must have the approval of the pastor and deacons.

Section 2–Church Polity
   The church polity not treated herein shall be governed by the principles set forth in *The New Directory for Baptist Churches* by Edward T. Hiscox.

Section 3–Pastor's Vacation and Salary
   A. The pastor shall have not less than three weeks paid vacation each year.
   B. The pastor's salary shall be reviewed and determined at least once a year, with consideration also being given to rising costs of living.

Section 4–Monetary Principles
   A. The systematic giving of money for the support of the work of the Lord is worship as well as duty. It must be kept on the plane of voluntary, freewill offerings, untarnished by any hope of material gain. All members are expected to give regular financial support to the church and to the advancement of the projects it shall sponsor. In determining the Lord's portion, we believe and affirm with the Scrip-

tures that at least one-tenth of one's income should be faithfully and cheerfully given by each one (2 Cor. 9:6, 7), and many can and should give more than the tithe, for all we have belongs to Christ (1 Chron. 29:14, 16; Acts 4:32-35). No monies shall be raised for the support of the church and its various activities by any but the Biblical plan of tithes, offerings and gifts.

B. A statement of each donor's account shall be given to him at the end of each year by the financial secretary. Numbered envelopes will be provided to enable proper records to be kept.

Section 5–Legal Provisions

A. This church shall have the right to own, buy or sell tangible properties, both real and personal, in its own name and through properly elected officers, when authorized by vote of the church.

B. No profit shall ever accrue to the benefit of any individuals from the assets, holdings or other transactions in which this corporation may become involved.

C. In the event of the dissolution of this corporation, all of its debts shall be fully satisfied. None of its assets or holdings shall be divided among the members or other individuals, but shall be irrevocably designated by corporate vote prior to dissolution to such other nonprofit religious corporations as are in agreement with the letter and spirit of the articles of faith adopted by this church, and in conformity with the requirements of the United States Internal Revenue Service Code of 1954 (Section 501 C-3).

Article XIII—Amendments and Bylaws

This constitution may be amended, altered or revised at any annual business meeting by a *three-fourths* vote of the members present and voting, provided such proposed changes shall have been submitted in writing not later than the October meeting preceding.

The church may adopt from time to time such bylaws in amplification hereof as may be necessary or desirable, and shall provide therein for amendment of the same.

APPENDIX A

Forms

No arbitrary forms for certificates, letters and similar documents are commonly used by Baptist churches. No legal requirements are involved in these forms. Each church is at liberty to prepare or purchase such certificates as it deems most suitable.

The following forms are suggested for the convenience of those who desire advice in these matters, and may be altered to meet local situations or personal preference.

Request for Letter of Dismission[1]

_____, 19_____

To the _____ Baptist Church

_____

(Address)

M _____, residing at _____

_____,

has requested to unite with us upon transfer of his (her) membership from your church. If this meets with your approval, we will appreciate receiving a suitable letter of dismission at your convenience.

_____

(Pastor or Clerk)

_____ Baptist Church

_____

(Address)

---

1. Available in printed form from Regular Baptist Press. Order RBP5501.

Letter of Dismission to Churches of Like Faith and Order[2]

To the _____ Baptist Church

_____

(Address)

Christian Greeting:

This certifies that _____ is a member of _____ Baptist Church in good and regular standing, and at his (her) own request is hereby dismissed from our fellowship to unite with you.

When _____ shall have been received by you, please inform us of this action and his (her) connection with us will cease.

May God's choicest blessing abide on _____ and on you.

By order and in behalf of the _____ Baptist Church, _____, 19_____

_____, Pastor   City _____

_____, Church Clerk   State _____

Notice of Dismission

For the purpose of aiding you to properly establish _____ in the life and work of your church, the following information is appended:

Attends public worship: Regularly _____ Occasionally _____
Attends prayer meeting: Regularly _____ Occasionally _____
Attends Sunday school _____ Other services _____
Gives to support of church _____ Missions _____
Official positions _____
Especially interested in _____

Certificate of Reception (to be returned to dismissing church)

This is to certify that _____

_____

(Address)

was received into the membership of the _____ Baptist Church on _____, 19_____

_____, Church Clerk

2. Form letters similar to the three included under this heading may be purchased at some bookstores. The three forms are attached and all sent to the church requesting the letter. The letters are attached to suitable stubs which are bound in permanent form and constitute a record for the dismissing church. Similar letters may be produced by the church if this is desired.

A printed letter of dismission is available from Regular Baptist Press. Order RBP5502. A printed certificate of reception is also available. Order RBP5504.

Letter of Dismission to Churches of Other Than Like Faith and Order[3]

Certificate of Membership

To Whom It May Concern:

This certifies that _____, a member of our church in good and regular standing, is hereby dismissed at his (her) own request, and is commended to the confidence and fellowship of sister churches.

Done by order and in behalf of the church.

Name of dismissing church _____

City and date _____

_____
(Church Clerk)

Letter of Commendation[4]

To Whom It May Concern:

This certifies that _____ is a member of our church in good and regular standing and is hereby commended to the confidence and fellowship of sister churches and fellow believers.

Name of church _____

City and date _____

Letter of Watchcare (Not Change of Membership)

To _____ Date _____

City _____

Dear Brethren in Christ:

_____ Baptist Church often has students and others who worship with us for an extended period, but who do not wish to move their memberships. Some may be planning to go to the mission field and desire to retain membership in their home churches, yet would like to be used of the Lord while in our city and area.

3. A printed form is available from Regular Baptist Press. Order RBP5503.
4. This letter does not dismiss a member, but conveys the church's introduction and commendation of a member who may be traveling or for other reasons be away from the home church temporarily and seeking fellowship in sister churches.
A printed form is available from Regular Baptist Press. Order RBP5505.

We are happy to assume a "watchcare" relationship to such persons who are of like precious faith and agree to our statement of faith and who are commended by their home church. On the part of the home church it involves simply a letter of commendation with the recommendation of Christian character and experience. On the part of the individual it involves assuming a similar faithfulness while here to that which they would follow in their home church, except that the tithe should continue to go to the home church. (Voluntary offerings here would be acceptable.) On our part, it would mean the granting of the various privileges of service within the church but with no power of vote. As a church and as pastor we would seek to minister to them in the same personal way we would to our membership in matters of counseling, visitation, care by pastoral calling when sick and other such matters.

(Mr.) (Mrs.) (Miss) _____ has expressed a desire to have such a relationship with this church. Would you kindly forward us your official church approval of this relationship, stating any information you may desire which would help us to assist or use the brother (or sister) above mentioned to the glory of God. Yours in Christ,

_____ Baptist Church

_____
(Pastor)

_____
(Clerk)

(The form below may be used for your convenience.)

_____ Baptist Church

_____
(Street)

_____
        (City)   (State)

Dear Brethren in Christ:
    We commend to you for your watchcare _____, and trust that the relationship may be one of mutual spiritual profit and blessing.
Additional information:
Faithfulness _____
Spiritual zeal _____
Any peculiar doctrinal view _____

Teaching experience: age group ____; years of experience _____
Music: choir ( )   instrumental ( )   other ( )
Other comments _____
Use other side for more lengthy comment if you desire.
Yours in Christ,
_____ Baptist Church

_____
(Pastor)

_____
(Clerk)

Call for an Ordination Council

The _____Baptist Church of
_____ to the
_____Baptist Church of
_____.

Dear Brethren:
    You are requested to send your pastor and two brethren to sit
with us in council on _____ in _____ to consider
the advisability of setting aside to the gospel ministry our Brother
_____, who is a member of our church. The council
will convene at _____ P.M.
    If the council acts favorably, the ordination service will be held
_____.

    Done by order and in behalf of the church.

_____
(City)

_____
(Date)

_____
(Church Clerk)
The following churches and individuals are invited:

Call for a Recognition Council

To the _____ Baptist Church of

_____

Dear Brethren:

A company of believers, having organized themselves into a Baptist church and desiring to have fellowship with other churches of like precious faith, hereby invites you to send your pastor and two brethren to sit in council with others on _____ in _____ to consider the propriety of recognizing said church as a Baptist church.

The service will begin at _____ P.M.

Done by order and in behalf of the church.

_____

(Name of church)

_____

(City)

_____

(Date)

_____

(Church Clerk)

The following churches and individuals are invited:

Call for an Advisory Council

The _____Baptist Church of
_____ to the
_____ Baptist Church of
_____.

Dear Brethren:

There being certain difficulties existing among us which hinder our testimony and threaten to disrupt our church, we invite you to send your pastor and two brethren to sit in council with others to hear both sides of the matter and give us your Christian advice.

The council will be held on _____ at _____ P.M.

Done by order and in behalf of the church.

_____
(Name of church)

_____
(City)

_____
(Date)

_____
(Church Clerk)

The following churches and individuals are invited:

Certificate of License[5]

This is to certify that at a meeting of the _____-_____ Baptist Church, _____, on the _____ day of _____ 19_____, having given evidence that he possesses gifts for the work of the gospel ministry,

_____

was licensed to preach the gospel as he may have opportunity, and to exercise his gifts in the work of the ministry.

This license shall be valid for one year from above date, at which time the license may be extended by vote of the church.

When acting as pastor of a Baptist church and authorized by that church so to do, he shall be considered eligible to administer the ordinances of baptism and the Lord's Supper, and to officiate at funerals and weddings, when compatible with the laws of the state.

_____

(Moderator)

_____

(Pastor)

_____

(Church Clerk)

5. A printed certificate is available from Regular Baptist Press. Order RBP5507.

APPENDIX B

Bibliography

Barlow, Fred M. *Vitalizing Your Sunday School Visitation*. Schaumburg, IL: Regular Baptist Press.

Cohen, Gary G. *Biblical Separation Defended*. Grand Rapids: Baker Book House.

Evans, William. *Personal Soul Winning*. Chicago: Moody Press.

Griffith, Earle G. *The Pastor as God's Minister*. Schaumburg, IL: Regular Baptist Press.

Hiscox, Edward T. *The Hiscox Guide for Baptist Churches*. Valley Forge, PA: Judson Press.

Hiscox, Edward T. *The New Directory for Baptist Churches*. Grand Rapids: Kregel Publications.

Lightner, Robert P. *Neoevangelicalism Today*. Schaumburg, IL: Regular Baptist Press.

Lumpkin, William L. *Baptist Confessions of Faith*. Valley Forge, PA: Judson Press.

Matthews, Reginald L. *Missionary Administration in the Local Church*. Schaumburg, IL: Regular Baptist Press.

Matthews, Reginald L. *The Ordination of Men Called of God to the Ministry of the Word*. Schaumburg, IL: Regular Baptist Press.

Mullins, Edgar Y. *Baptist Beliefs*. Valley Forge, PA: Judson Press.

Murdoch, J. Murray. *Portrait of Obedience: The Biography of Robert T. Ketcham*. Schaumburg, IL: Regular Baptist Press.

Pardee, William H. *Baptism: Its Importance, Its Subjects, Its Mode*. Schaumburg, IL: Regular Baptist Press.

Pickering, Ernest. *Biblical Separation: The Struggle for a Pure Church*. Schaumburg, IL: Regular Baptist Press.

Reese, J. Irving. *A Guide for Organizing and Conducting a Baptist Church*. Elyria, OH: J. Irving Reese Publications.

Torbet, Robert G. *A History of Baptists* (revised). Valley Forge, PA: Judson Press.

Wagner, Charles U. *The Pastor: His Life and Work*. Schaumburg, IL: Regular Baptist Press.